SMART MARKETING FOR LIFE COACHES

HOW TO USE PERSONAL BRANDING TO AMPLIFY EARNINGS AND SIMPLIFY SUCCESS

By Judy Kirkland, CLC and Susan Weaver, CLC

Published by:

THE LIVEWELL INSTITUTE

www.thelivewellinstitute.com

THE LIVEWELL INSTITUTE

The LiveWell Institute
PO Box 461
Herndon, VA 20172-0461 U.S.A.
www.thelivewellinstitute.com

Published by: The LiveWell Institute

This book is intended to provide assistance in establishing a core coaching business based on years of experience and written by Certified Life Coaches. The book does not guarantee a particular outcome, as each individual user must create their own successful results.

Printed in the United States of America on Acid-Free Paper
10 9 8 7 6 5 4 3 2 1

ISBN: 978-0-9910592-4-9
Library of Congress Control Number: 2017941360

BUSINESS & ECONOMICS: Mentoring & Coaching
Personal Success
Marketing / General

CONGRATULATIONS!

You've become a life coach.

Now, how will you build a thriving practice?

You know how to begin coaching, but do you know how to begin *marketing?* For many life coaches, practice-building can be a challenge, especially since using a traditional business marketing template won't work for life coaches. That's because your practice isn't a business, it's *you* ... and you are unique.

You have different traits, strengths, values and experiences than any other life coach on earth. If you try to promote your practice using a template that works for other types of businesses or even other life coaches, you're virtually guaranteed to spend money on marketing tactics that simply don't work for your unique practice. You'll also find yourself trying to promote yourself in ways that are uncomfortable because they don't fit with who you are and where you shine.

Throw away the cookie cutter! As a life coach, you know that self-awareness is a powerful filter for making decisions about what does and doesn't matter. It's also a powerful tool for deciding what goals to set and how to go about achieving them. Now, instead of a cookie-cutter marketing plan, you're going to learn how to use a form of self-awareness – personal branding – to define the goals, tactics and budget that will be most beneficial for *your unique life coaching practice*. Plus, to build your step-by-step marketing program, we're going to use something that's very familiar to you: the same SMART strategies you use to help your clients set and achieve goals.

So, instead of trying to *attempt all tactics possible,* you'll learn how to develop a personal brand that filters out what *won't work* so you can focus on tactics that perfectly match:

YOUR MARKETPLACE: You provide a very personal service. Your best marketing efforts are likely to come from personal interaction (such as referrals and word-of-mouth) or personal lead generation (speaking engagements and networking) rather than from mass marketing tactics like radio or TV ads. You'll learn how to use your personal brand to match your own natural marketing strengths with the best tactics for connecting with your specific audience.

YOUR BANDWIDTH: How much time can you realistically allot for marketing? If your practice hasn't yet become your sole source of income, then coaching, family life and working your other job may not leave room for time-intensive tactics like joining networking groups that meet monthly or even weekly. Here, you'll learn how to use your personal brand to define activities that will give you the biggest impact from the time you *can* invest.

... BUDGET: How much can you spend at this point? Eventually, you might want to invest in a professionally-produced brochure or a paid search program. Right now, however, you may not have the budget. We'll show you how to use your personal brand to decide what's comfortable, and what free and nearly-free tactics you might use to jump-start growth.

Before we get started developing your brand-based life coach marketing program, let's take a quick overview of the components that will make up your plan:

1. **Personal Branding:** who you are as a person (strengths and traits), how you're different from other life coaches, how you change clients' lives.

2. **Basic Toolkit:** step-by-step guidance for creating your website and key marketing materials.

3. **Engagement:** creating the right value propositions, pricing and offers to engage different audiences, including prospects, clients and former clients.

4. **Networking:** investing in the right personal and professional activities to generate – and develop – leads and referrals for coaching.

5. **Social Media:** how to get and stay visible on Facebook, LinkedIn and other sites; plus specific types of coaching content to use on each.

6. **Events:** how to create, plan, promote and successfully present free, lead-generating events plus profit-making seminars – live or online.

7. **Search:** how to optimize free organic search engine rankings and use paid search programs.

8. **Action Plan:** defining your tactics, planning your budget and creating an easy month-by-month list of small, SMART goals that can generate big growth for your life-coaching practice.

Every life coach's plan will include all these categories of marketing. The *difference* is that you'll be using your personal brand to filter what specific activities you will do within each category. This is how you'll arrive at a promotion plan that's perfectly aligned with your personal strengths and professional goals. It's also how you'll be able to market your practice effectively even if you can't invest a large amount of time or money right now.

Before we begin, let's look at how this guide works. First, we'll show you how to develop your own personal brand. Next, we'll discuss a wide variety of tactics that work for life coaches – and we'll show you how to use your brand to decide which of these tactics will work best for you. Finally, we'll make it easy for you to pull the tactics you've selected into a simple, step-by-step SMART marketing plan – one that you absolutely have the strengths, bandwidth and budget to execute successfully.

Now, let's get started!

TABLE OF CONTENTS

Page

SECTION I: PERSONAL BRANDING 1

SECTION 2: BASIC TOOLKIT 9

SECTION 3: ENGAGEMENT 29

SECTION 4: NETWORKING 37

SECTION 5: SOCIAL MEDIA 53

SECTION 6: EVENTS 65

SECTION 7: SEARCH 73

SECTION 8: YOUR SMART LIFE COACH MARKETING PLAN 79

ABOUT THE AUTHORS 85

ABOUT THE LIVEWELL INSTITUTE 87

INDEX 89

SECTION 1:
PERSONAL BRANDING

YOUR PERSONAL BRAND

In marketing any business, a brand matters. The brand communicates what the business stands for, how it's different from other brands and its unique value to its unique audience. Businesses that take the time to develop – and live – their brands enjoy dramatically greater success than businesses that don't spend time defining their brands. Why?

Because a brand makes a business more visible and valuable. It lets people know what kind of product and customer experience to expect. These factors pre-market the business so that actual advertising and promotion drive better results, faster. A strong brand makes customers happy to spend more for the product. A clear brand also improves the success and lowers the cost of marketing by serving as a filter for understanding *in advance* what kind of tactics will and won't work for the business. As a life coach, your business isn't a product: *your business is you*. That's why a personal brand is the starting point for marketing your practice most successfully.

What is a personal brand?

A personal brand is everything you say and do. It's how you appear and how you behave. In short, it is the outward reflection of the story you want to tell about yourself and how you want clients to experience your coaching.

> For your personal brand to do this, it has to be ***yours***. You can't 'paste on' behaviors or copy what other coaches do or say.

Developing a true personal brand takes some time because it addresses not just your coaching practice, but every aspect of your life. The LiveWell Institute's *Plan BE Program* takes you through this process and helps you begin to use your personal brand to address everything from relationships and finances, to living the life you've always wanted.

Right now, however, our goal is to empower you to develop a personal brand you can start using immediately to promote your coaching practice.

Personal branding quickstart: Your comfort zone

Let's start by identifying your comfort zone. Far from being a bad, lazy or boring place, your comfort zone is a good place: it's where you can find a whole suite of strengths. It's where you feel energized enough – and safe enough – to create new strategies.

Thus, your comfort zone is actually a powerfully positive space. When you're in your comfort zone, you're not only comfortable, you're highly effective – and confident – in using strengths you *already have* to achieve goals you've always wanted.

Imagine the difference when you begin to use your comfort zone as your filter for making choices about how you look, what you say and how you behave! You'll always be working from strengths, and they'll be strengths you already have so no energy gets siphoned off trying to paste on someone else's strengths. These are your *genuine* strengths, so you'll feel comfortable every step of the way.

DEFINE YOUR COMFORT ZONE

1. **What are your strengths?** Brainstorm as many strengths as you can. Strengths can be big or small – anything from listening and solving problems to creating systems, being practical, being spiritual, etc.

2. **What kinds of situations make you feel most comfortable and confident?** Again, brainstorm different types of settings and situations.

3. **What types of things give you the greatest satisfaction?** Try to be specific. For example, don't just write 'Helping People.' Write the type of person and the type of help you most enjoying giving.

4. **How is your coaching different?** This could be anything from your approach or view of coaching, to the fact that you've traveled extensively or have specific coaching certifications.

Now, go back to your answers in each section. Shorten each answer to a word or phrase and write them into the comfort zone grid on the next page.

YOUR COMFORT ZONE

STRENGTHS	SATISFACTION
COMFORT/CONFIDENCE	DIFFERENTIATORS

This is your comfort zone and your starting point for developing a personal brand you can use to:

- Choose marketing tactics that play to your specific strengths and where you feel most comfortable and confident
- Structure your practice around situations that give you the greatest satisfaction
- Feel more comfortable and confident in situations where you may not naturally feel at ease (e.g., in networking or public speaking)
- Use your strengths and differentiators to create messaging about your practice

FROM COMFORT ZONE TO PERSONAL BRAND

The comfort zone grid you've completed shows the traits and strengths that are part of your personal brand. Now, the secret is to use these traits and strengths to create messaging that expresses what your personal brand is and *why it matters*. Here's how ...

Expand each strength and differentiator listed in your comfort zone grid. Do this by using the word because: e.g., "Because I am practical ... my clients can immediately apply the ideas we come up with in coaching sessions."

BECAUSE I ...	MY CLIENTS ...

The statements above are the raw material for what to say about your practice. With a little polishing, they become what you use on your website, brochure and elevator pitch (discussed in later chapters). You can also begin to internalize these messages so they come naturally (and sound conversational, not salesy) when you're talking with people casually or at professional functions.

The final step for your quick-start personal brand is to define it 'in action.' The traits in your comfort zone grid are not your actual brand. They are the *ingredients*. Think about eggs, flour, butter and milk: combine them in one way and you get cookies; in another way you get a cake, or pancakes, or popovers or a soufflé. It is the way you define your brand traits that will define your personal brand.

BRAND TRAIT	HOW IT LOOKS	HOW IT SOUNDS	HOW IT BEHAVES
List each key strength and differentiator from your comfort zone grid below.	Write how each trait can be reflected in the appearance of your website design, your coaching materials and your own image.	Write how each trait can be reflected in how you speak and write (e.g. pleasant, enthusiastic, practical, positive, clear, calm, etc.).	Write how to live each trait. For instance, if one of your traits is being respectful, what will (and won't) demonstrate this?

Again, this is a very simple 'quick start' to personal branding. By going through these exercises you create a good filter for what story you want to tell about yourself and your coaching practice – and the messages and behaviors that will be most effective in telling that story.

In the following sections we'll look at how you can begin to tell this story using tactics ranging from your website to events. But before you begin actively promoting your practice, you need to develop a basic toolkit. Let's look at what goes in it.

PERSONAL BRAND + SMART GOALS

As a life coach, you know the best way to achieve goals is to make sure those goals are SMART:

- **SPECIFIC**
- **MEASURABLE**
- **ACTIONABLE**
- **REALISTIC**
- **TIME-DEFINED**

So, in addition to using your personal brand to develop your marketing plan, we're going to show you how to put that plan into action using a series of SMART goals. Personal brand plus SMART goals – this is the unique approach that can help you amplify your earnings *and* simplify that success.

SECTION 2:
BASIC TOOLKIT

CHECKLIST

The tools are useful to virtually every life coach. Some, like business cards, are essential. Others, like brochures, may be tools you don't need right away. In the following pages, we'll look more closely at each of these tools and provide tips and 'how-to' guidance on creating them for your own life coaching practice.

- Business bio
- Business card
- Elevator pitch
- 25-word business description
- Website
- Brochure and/or flyer
- Press release

YOUR BUSINESS BIO

As a coach, it's a good idea to include a business biography in your basic toolkit. You may need it immediately for your brochure or website, and you may find it handy if you're asked to speak or serve on a committee. Like defining your brand, writing your business bio is an excellent way to promote your strengths and differentiators.

Length: 99% of the time, all you need is a short paragraph

> Your business bio is not a resumé. It is not a dating profile. It should not tell your life story. Instead, its purpose is to quickly frame-up your professional experience and credentials so people can choose you as a coach *with confidence.*

Dos and Don'ts for Writing Your Bio

- **Write it in the third person.** "Amy Winters is a Certified Life Coach ..." vs. "I am a ..."
- **Define what will make *your* audience feel confident** about choosing you as a coach. Ideas include:
  - How long you've been coaching (or years of experience that led to your coaching career)
  - Where you earned your coaching certification
  - Notable achievements: type of coaching certification, published articles, speaking engagements, awards
  - Professional affiliations: memberships and board positions
- **Focus on what is relevant to *coaching*.** Don't list every job you've ever had or what you studied in college *unless* it led to/contributed to your credentials as a coach.
- **Keep personal information professional.** Remember, this is a business bio and it's *short.* Avoid personal information about you, your family and hobbies. If you are interested in developing a local coaching practice, you might want to include a last sentence in your bio that mentions where you live.

SAMPLE: *Amy Winters is a Certified Life Coach who specializes in helping women make fresh starts after divorce, the death of a loved one, health issues or other life-changing events. In addition to her training as a coach, Amy draws on years of front-line HR experience helping employees defuse conflicts and identify practical ways to achieve greater success and satisfaction at work and in personal life. She is currently working on ICF mentor coach certification. While Amy is based in Washington, DC, she also works with clients across the nation via Facetime and Skype.*

BUSINESS CARD

We can bump our smartphones together and – zap! – we've shared contact information. We can even say, "You can find me on LinkedIn." But we still need business cards. Here's why:

- Business cards support your image as a life coaching *professional* who is running a true practice vs. a hobby or sideline.
- Business cards give people an immediate sense of your brand – colors, style, strength, professionalism, creativity.
- A good business card also serves as a physical leave-behind that reminds the person of you and what you may have talked about.
- Even in non-business settings you'll find people carry business cards with them.

What to include

- Your name and business name, logo and certifications
- Phone and email
- Website address (you might even consider putting a QR code on the back of your card that can be 'snapped' with a smartphone camera to take someone right to your website. There are free QR code generators you can download to do this)
- Social media icons/social media profiles
- Design that reflects your brand (fonts, colors, spacing, etc. that support your brand)

Your logo

If you don't have a logo you'll need to have one designed or design it yourself. Even if you design the logo yourself we recommend using a professional graphic designer to create the correct file formats for printing.

Here are some options for creating a logo:

- **Design the logo yourself.** This is a good idea if you know exactly what you want and can communicate your idea with a drawing or create it on the computer. Even if you create the logo yourself it's a good idea to have a professional graphic designer create logo print files to ensure correct color, resolution, formats and printing.

- **Use a website that designs logos.** Seaech 'logo design' on Google to find websites that can assist you in creating a logo. The advantage is they are reasonably priced and do a pretty good job. One disadvantage is that the logo may not be as customized in terms of brand identity as compared to working closely with a professional graphic designer.

- **Use a professional graphic designer.** This is the most expensive option, but you will have greater ability to reflect your personalized brand identity by working one-on-one with a graphic designer.

Create your business cards

- **Size and format.** Typical business cards are 3.5" x 2" and can be positioned horizontally or vertically. Additional size options include: square; slightly oversized; rounded corners; and other odd shapes. Size and format should be determined prior to designing the card.

- **Design options.** There are a few ways to have your business card designed:

  - *Do it yourself* – designing your own business card is a great idea but be sure your print-ready files are up to par with what your printer needs in terms of art file creation and resolution. If you're not sure what that means it would be a good idea to have a professional graphic designer create the print files.

  - *Use a professional graphic designer* – this will cost more but is your best bet for communicating your brand identity and ensuring proper file set-up for printing.

  - *Use an online printer* – look for templates to help design your cards. Our favorite is MOO Printing (www.moo.com/us).

  - *Use a local printer* – many printers have in-house graphic design capability. This may be a good fit if you're having your cards printed locally.

- **Printing.** Options for printing your business cards:

  - *Use an online printer* – prices tend to be extremely reasonable and the quality is pretty good. Of course you get what you pay for, and there's a chance that color accuracy or registration may be off a bit with no recourse for correction. Typically, online printers will print 4-color (CMYK) on both sides of the card as standard. We use MOO Printing (www.moo.com/us) and have been very happy with the results.

  - *Use a local printer* – there's a difference between small and medium-size printers vs. large printers, and each has certain types of jobs that 'fit' their equipment. Find a small or medium-size printer to handle your business card order. Ask about 'digital' printing for small runs and compare prices between a couple different vendors. Local printers will offer a wider variety of paper choices – including colors and textures – that you won't be able to get with an online printer, and you'll have more control over your job start to finish.

- **Choice of paper.** It's the paper and not the ink that makes a printed piece look 'shiny', 'smooth', or 'flat'. There are the 3 basic types of finishes:
  - Gloss – a coated stock with a shiny finish that reflects light
  - Dull, Matte or Silk – a coated stock with a soft sheen that does not reflect light
  - Uncoated – a flat finish with no coating – does not reflect light
- **Paper weight.** Business cards need to be a minimum of 80# cover stock, with 100# cover weight or heavier preferred. The heavier weight adds credibility to the 'feel' of your business card.
- **Quantity.** When setting estimates and comparing printing costs, be sure to request a few different quantites (ie. #250/#500/#1000). Depending on the printer, print method being used, and the printer's setup, the cost per unit typically decreases as quantity increases, and may vary greatly between wendors.

ELEVATOR PITCH

As we'll see later in the Networking section, it's important to have a good 10-second answer to the question, "What do you do?" We'll also look at examples of how to use your elevator pitch not just to present yourself as a life coach, but to open a conversation about life coaching and its value.

This 10-second introduction is called your Elevator Pitch. The best elevator pitches are (obviously) short and memorable.

You could simply respond, "I'm a life coach." Frankly, not a lot of people know what a life coach is so you need to be ready to explain not just what a life coach does but also how life changes for people who have a life coach.

Another option is to create an elevator pitch that presents 'the end vision' of how life changes *first*. Let's look at some examples from other professions:

The obvious response to "What do you do"	Presenting the end vision first
I'm a financial planner. I help with taxes, investments and retirement.	I help people sleep at night so they can dream. I'm a financial planner.
I'm a social worker. I work with at-risk children.	I rekindle hope in children who have lost it. I'm a social worker.

Presenting the vision first creates a far more memorable impression. For a life coach, this approach also gives you the opportunity to elevate what you do. That's important because people who don't understand life coaching may think it's a frivolous, light-weight service. In fact, there are so many reasons to go with a memorable, present-the-end-first approach. The only reason *not* to is if it's so outside your comfort zone that you'll feel awkward. If that's the case, stick with "I'm a life coach" and be prepared to follow up with why that matters.

The following exercise is designed to help you define why your own brand of life coaching matters. You can use this exercise to create your 'end vision' elevator pitch, or to follow up on your more standard "I'm a life coach" response.

EXERCISE: Develop Your Elevator Pitch

Every life coach is different. You take a different approach, focus on a different audience, have a different personality or philosophy. What's important is to use this ***process*** rather than the actual examples we've provided. Using the statements below as examples, brainstorm ideas in each category. List your ideas in the right-hand column.

WHAT DO YOU DO? Remember, if you want to say "I'm a life coach," that's fine. Use this part of the exercise to prepare what you'll say as a follow on. Examples include: • I help people figure out goals/steps • I help people get unstuck • I hold people accountable for doing things • I help people stop being fearful • I give people the power of self-awareness • I help people define the 'goal behind the goal'	______________________ ______________________ ______________________ ______________________ ______________________ ______________________ ______________________ ______________________ ______________________ ______________________ ______________________
HOW DOES LIFE CHANGE BECAUSE OF WHAT YOU DO? *EXAMPLE: Go back to what you listed above and say to yourself, "Because I hold people accountable, they _____"* • Find out how smart they really are • Discover power and opportunities they didn't imagine existed • Feel more satisfied with life, more confident and in control • Have more energy to make changes/ go after success and thrive **This is the END VISION**	______________________ ______________________ ______________________ ______________________ ______________________ ______________________ ______________________ ______________________ ______________________ ______________________ ______________________

Now let's use some of the END VISION ideas to experiment with your elevator pitch:

I show people how to turn self-awareness into satisfying new success. I'm a life coach.

I help people 'unstick' their energy, and develop their confidence and power to thrive. I'm a life coach.

You see what we're doing here? We're picking up ideas from our answers and combining them in different ways. Your own answers will be different. Just keep moving the phrases around and you're sure to hit on an elevator pitch that is the perfect fit for you and your own unique life coaching practice.

25-WORD BUSINESS DESCRIPTION

Having a short business description is handy in a variety of situations, including:

- Your LinkedIn business description
- Use for local business directories (Yelp, Local, etc.)
- Part of your bio for speaking engagements, webinars, etc.
- Company profile for your listing in membership organizations
- The 'about me' paragraph in letters or emails to prospects people have referred

Avoid the biggest mistake: Your business description needs to be short and there is no room for 'warm up words.' Warm-up words talk about HOW you do something vs. WHAT you do. Example: *"As a life coach I use a personalized approach in helping people ..."* A phrase like that eats up half of your 25 words and we still don't know what you do. Other warm-up words to avoid: *"Since 2010, I've been helping ..."* Years in practice may be relevant but it is a secondary message useful for establishing credibility vs. stating what you do.

Here's what *should* be included:

1. Your name/the name of your business
2. Your coaching niche (an approach, a particular audience, etc.)
3. The end benefit to your clients

Let's look at an example:

BrandEquity Coaching helps you develop your personal Brand Equity (BE) so you can use strengths you already have to live the life you've always dreamed.

Name of the practice

Niche: using brand as the coaching platform

Benefit

EXACTLY 25 WORDS

EXERCISE: Write Your Business Description

1. **Write the name of your practice:**

   ____

2. **List three different ways to describe your coaching niche:**
   For example, these all might be different ways to describe the same life coaching practice: I help people take control of their lives ... I specialize in work-life balance ... I help people develop new 'life control' skills ...

   ____

   ____

   ____

   Now, of these, pick the idea that seems strongest to you. Whittle it down to as short a phrase as you can and write it here:

   ____

3. **List three different ways to describe the end benefit to your clients:**
   For instance, continuing with the example above, end benefits might be: ... so they can focus on what matters ... so they can stop settling for less ... so they can trade 'default' existence for richer, intentional lives...

   ____

   ____

   ____

   Again, pick the best of these ideas. Whittle it down to as short a phrase as you can and write it here: ____

4. **Now combine the three elements:**

   [Name] ____

   [Niche, from #2] ____

   [End Benefit, from #3] so ____

5. **Just keep working with your statement to weed out warm-up words and whittle it down to its final 25-word length:**

   ____

   ____

WEBSITE

As a professional life coach, you absolutely need a website. You don't, however, necessarily need a large, expensive website brimming with videos, interactive content, shopping cart, etc. – especially if you're just starting out. So, in this section of the Toolkit, let's look at the basics of how to create a simple website for your practice.

The 3 Basic Parts of Your Website

1. **The URL.** Short and memorable is best. It's also good if you can make your name or the name of your life coaching practice the URL: *ChrisSmithGoalCoach.com* or *GoalCoach.com*. If those domain names are already taken, try adding a location: *GoalCoachLocalCity.com*.

   Domain names range in price and typically are under $20/year. Source for URLs: *www.GoDaddy.com*

2. **Hosting.** Web hosting is a service that makes your website accessible via the Internet.

   There are many free hosting providers, but – for life coaches – do-it-yourself hosting probably doesn't make sense. Instead, you want to go with a service that will set up website features for you like an email address for your business and the ability to collect emails from prospects and clients, and send auto-response messages.

   Often, hosting is offered as part of a package that includes a website template, hosting and technical support. This is a great way to get started and companies like Google and GoDaddy offer these packages starting at around $20/month.

3. **The website itself.** You can create your own, or use templates from the many free website sources on the Internet. Google offers small business packages as well. Or, you can have your website custom created by a professional design or web firm.

   Obviously, having a professional create your site is easier – the designer knows how to translate your brand into the right look, tone, and functionality for your website and does everything including making your website live.

   A professional designer, however, is the most expensive option. If you're just starting out, it's fine to go with a template. Just be sure that the template, photos and content you put into the site reflect your brand so it looks different from other sites and so it looks like *you*. Go back to your personal brand traits to make sure everything from the font to the color palette is right for the story you want to tell about yourself and your practice.

Creating Your Website

Templates and packaged websites typically start you off with a 5-page website. Remember that the goal of a good website is to keep people from leaving too soon. In fact, if a lot of people come to your website (sounds good!) but then 'bounce' away too quickly after landing on your home page, this will lower your search rankings (this is bad).

Website Rule #1: Don't spill your candy in the lobby

Many life coaches make the mistake of trying to put *everything* on the home page. Visitors to the site get overwhelmed: suddenly, life coaching looks hard and expensive and time-consuming. Instead, think of the home page as a magazine cover: It should show a taste of what's inside and invite you to go inside and find out more about the content that interests you.

Website Rule #2: People read just 300 characters a minute

Good writing can actually cover a lot of ground in 300 characters. The problem is the typical visitor only spends *about 15 seconds* on a page before clicking deeper into the site or bouncing out. That means you have just 75 characters to engage people and get them to stick with you a bit longer.

Back to the magazine cover example: Don't risk everything on a long paragraph of text since the first 75 characters might not be strong enough to make a connection. Instead make sure your home page offers a lot of entry paths into your site – links to click, snippets of text, captions, photos, etc. that are all hyperlinked to other pages in your site.

Website Rule #3: You're creating a funnel

A website is not an online brochure. It is not a booklet that gets read sequentially from the home page to the contact page with the visitor stopping at all the pages on the site. In fact, the way that search engines work, more people may arrive at your website via the testimonials page rather than the home page. Each page must function as a stand-alone message. *Each page must funnel people toward an **engagement step**:*

- Call you
- Email you
- Sign up for your newsletter or report
- Follow you on Facebook
- Join your LinkedIn network

On the following page is a roadmap for what content to put on each page of your website, and how to funnel visitors to engage on each and every page.

WEB PAGE	CONTENT	WHERE CONTENT LINKS
HOME	25-word business description (see page 19)	ABOUT page
	Quote from a client	TESTIMONIAL page
	Special Offer (see ENGAGEMENT section)	CONTACT page
	Sign-up: Report, Newsletter, etc.	CONTACT page
	Photos with captions that highlight different ways in which you can help clients	SERVICES page
	How to contact you: phone, email	Phone number also links to CONTACT page; Email links to a pop-up email message ready to fill in and send.
	Logo, name of your business	
	Banner photo that reflects your brand	
	Icons: Follow us on FB, LI, YouTube, etc.	
ABOUT	Your bio, certifications, qualifications. Include a link near these to testimonials	TESTIMONIAL page
	Your general approach to coaching, what the experience is like, the kinds of things you've helped clients achieve	SERVICES page
	Phone and email contact info	CONTACT page and email message form
	Invitation to join your LinkedIn network/FB pages	LinkedIn/FB pages
SERVICES	Details about sessions: length of typical session, interaction, goal-setting and follow up for next session	TESTIMONIAL page
	Coaching formats: Do you offer phone coaching? Group coaching? Do you provide seminars for businesses or medical practices? Etc.	CONTACT page
	Special packages. E.g., multi-session discounts, fixed-price/fixed-session packages that focus on a particular goal (see ENGAGEMENT section)	CONTACT page
	List examples of how you can help	CONTACT page
TESTIMONIALS	Client quotes – but don't just feature the quote – give each a very short subhead that summarizes the benefit of life coaching (e.g., 'Less stress; more satisfaction')	CONTACT page
	Mention availability of special packages	SERVICES page
	Invitation to follow your Facebook page	Facebook
CONTACT	Short sentence or two inviting people to call you and try a free introductory session	
	Your name, business name, phone, email, website address, etc.	Email links to form
	Newsletter sign up, free report request	

Website Assessment Tool for Life Coaches

Is your website well-branded? Once you have the right content and engagement funnel, the final step is to make sure your website reflects your brand. Here is a rating tool to help you do that.

Rate each aspect of your website using the scale below:

0 =	Missing or poorly executed
1 =	Covered, but not compelling (e.g., you sound like any life coach, or life coaching sounds *nice* to have vs. *need* to have)
2 =	Covered and compelling but needs to be more concise
3 =	Covered, compelling and concise

	SCORE
1. **Professionalism and quality of the site:** The website loads quickly. It uses quality photographs. There are no typos or grammatical errors. The pages look inviting and easy to read. Navigation is clear and quick. Site content is up to date.	
2. **Presentation of your practice:** There is a clear, concise definition of your practice and the value proposition (see ENGAGEMENT section). The site is in no way generic – you could not substitute the name of any other life coach and have the site still work because it reflects your own voice, your own views, your own unique strengths and differentiators.	
3. **Connection with your audience:** Photos on the website reflect your audience. You demonstrate an understanding of pain points and aspirations. This may include explaining how what you do aligns with trends and concerns in today's stressful environment. Your tone/word choice is appropriate for that audience.	
4. **Credibility:** The site includes testimonials, awards, your certifications, presentation of your expertise and experience, etc. You use testimonials and text to highlight 'past performance' and show its specific value: before/after, increased satisfaction, achievement of a specific goal, etc.	
5. **Funnel:** Each page includes multiple links to other areas of the website. All pages urge the visitor to contact you. There are engagement options other than calling you to set up an appointment (e.g., sign up for newsletter, follow you on Facebook, join your LinkedIn network, etc.).	

By using this tool to assess your site, you will see where weaknesses exist. Once you've done the assessment yourself, you might have a friend use the tool to assess your site. This helps you double-check that your site is communicating the way you *think* it is. While the goal is to have a '3' rating in each section, focus *first* on fixing any areas with a '0' or '1' rating.

YOUR BROCHURE

First, do you even need a brochure?

Not every life coach does, especially those who are just getting started. Below is a quick checklist of when it is valuable to have a brochure IF:

✓ You are doing public speaking and would like to have a handout about your practice.

✓ You need something to provide when people ask you for more information.

✓ You want to position your practice as well-established and businesslike (this is especially helpful in approaching referral partners like hospitals or business organizations).

✓ You would like a piece that relieved you of the need to explain who you are and what you do.

What kind of brochure do you need?

Format	**Best Uses**	**Best Type of Content to Include**
Brochure 11" x 8.5" / folded into thirds	• Handing out one-on-one • Including in presentation materials • Mailing with a letter • Establishing credibility	Why choose you as a life coach: who you are, your credentials, what people say about you – call to action to find out more.
Flyer 8.5" x 11" / flat / 2-sided	• Posting as a PDF to download from your website • Sending as an email attachment • Using as a handout	Details your process, answers questions about "why life coaching" and "how does it work?" – call to action to sign up for a first session, free.
Buckslip Approx. 3.5" x 9" / 2-sided	• Using in larger quantities as a handout • Leaving with referral partners • Including in a promotional mailing • Posting on community bulletin boards	A special offer or coaching package – call to action to sign up for the offer now.

How do you choose a format?

It's always best to work with a design professional who can create a brochure just for you. If you don't have the budget for that at first, a template can work as long as you use the work we did at the outset to choose colors, photos, fonts and messaging that reflects your specific brand.

There are many sources for brochure templates. Microsoft Word contains ready-to-use templates. Printers like VistaPrint offer templates. Google 'brochure templates' and you'll find plenty of sources for templates, many of them free.

What content goes into your brochure?

The content that goes into your brochure is determined by your brand, differentiators and key talking points. There are, however, certain elements that belong in every life coach's brochure. These elements include your photo, testimonials, contact information and a call to action. Below is one example of how these elements might be presented in a flyer.

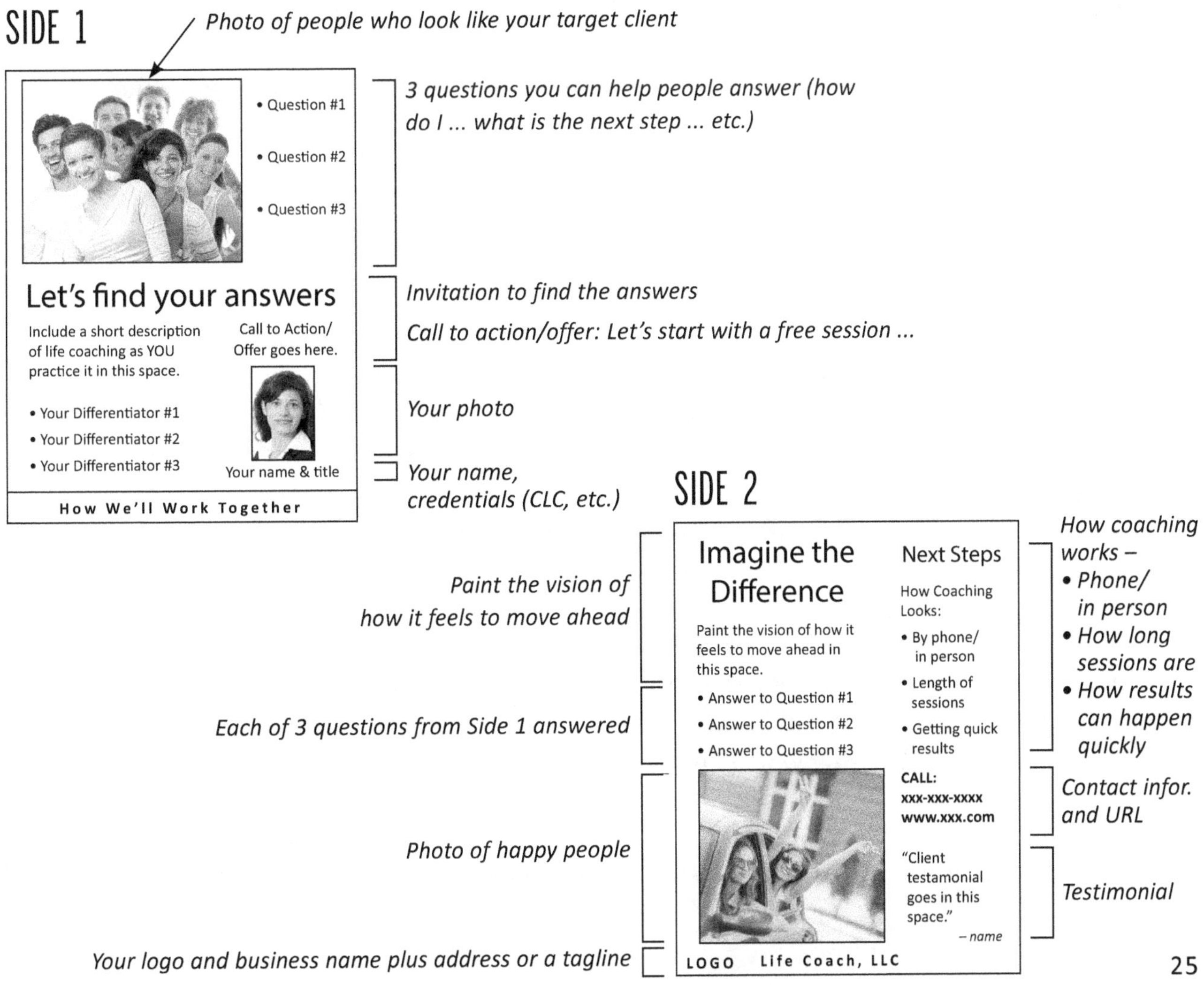

PRESS RELEASE

Press releases are a very efficient way to keep your practice visible. They also help raise the credibility and perceived value of life coaching. You can use press releases to share any kind of news about you, your practice or life coaching itself. There are many opportunities for using press releases, including to:

- Announce an upcoming speaking engagement or event.
- Mark a milestone anniversary for your practice.
- Announce a new engagement (not with individual clients, but something like: The LocalCity Medical Practice has engaged Chris Smith to provide coaching to help patients follow through with making lifestyle changes for better health ...').
- Share news about new certifications or services you offer.
- Call attention to a trend or challenge that life coaching can help address. Tie this to timely news such as people not wanting traditional retirements or college grads having a difficult time differentiating themselves in a competitive job market.
- Highlight something you've been recognized for (an award, publishing an article, etc.).
- Recognize others (e.g., "SoulCoaching recognizes the important work being done by SuchAndSuch Organization and invites LocalCity businesses to join in supporting ..." "The LocalCity school district has just implemented a program to teach goal setting ...").

Here are few ways that life coaches can use press releases:

- **Online press releases:** When you post a press release online, it has the potential to be picked up by bloggers and search engines. Your visibility can be even higher if you link to and from the online press release (i.e., press release includes a link to your website and your website and social media pages include links to the press release). There are a number of free online PR sites, but if you have a particularly important or high-profile release to issue, it might be worth using a paid online PR service such as PRWeb or PRNewswire.
- **Press releases (mailed or sent as email attachments):** You can send them to prospects, clients and past clients to share what you're up to. You can send them to editors at local newspapers and TV/radio stations along with a cover letter suggesting that you could provide further information on the topic that would be valuable to their audience.
- **On your website:** Like testimonials from clients, summaries of your press releases are important for validating that you're active and engaged in your field.

Basic Press Release Format

The following format is based on the requirements for PRWeb.com. This is an especially useful format because it includes the summary. This makes it very easy for bloggers to pick up the summary you've written verbatim, which is great for spreading the word and for becoming visible to search engines.

TITLE: 80 Characters (typically includes your name or practice name)

SUMMARY: 300 Characters

LEAD INs: Immediate release
Date
Where you are issuing the release (typically where your practice is based)

BODY: **300-400 words, written in 3rd person.** Never use 'I' or 'we' because your content will get dismissed as promotional rather than news or information. Many press release services won't accept copy that features personal pronouns unless they are part of quotations.

At least one hyperlink to your website. If you have the option, DO NOT link to the homepage. Instead, link to About or Testimonials. Instead of going to your homepage and bounding off, visitors who arrive on one of these other pages tend to stick there a little longer. They also tend to click to other pages, such as the homepage. This is important in getting more time with potential clients and raising your organic search rankings.

At least one quote. If you just have one quote, it should be from you. It's also a good idea to include quotes from others. For instance, if a medical practice is referring patients to you, a quote from one of the doctors or the office manager increases the credibility and newsworthiness of the press release. Be sure to cite the person's full name, title, and organization. Again, this is important for search visibility.

About your practice. Use your 25-word business description here.

CONTACT: **Your name**
Email
Phone
Website

END: Type: --END--

SAMPLE PRESS RELEASE

GoalCoach Chris Smith to Offer 'Career Pivot' Advice at LocalCity Chamber of Commerce Meeting

For people ready to trade jobs they do for jobs they love, GoalCoach Chris Smith will share surprisingly simple 'pivot strategies' for making career- and life-changing transformations. RSVP to attend the LocalCity Chamber of Commerce's September 15th luncheon at Mayler's Café: 123-444-5678.

Local City, CA, July 1, YEAR – LocalCity GoalCoach Chris Smith helps people break free from the habits and misconceptions that keep them stuck in jobs they've stopped loving. Smith helps clients use heightened self-awareness to define how they want to feel at work and translates this into specific types of careers. Smith will explain how to use small, easily attainable goal-setting exercises to land a new job and create a new life. Smith will share her approach plus case studies of clients' career pivots at the LocalCity Chamber of Commerce's upcoming luncheon: September 15 from 11:30 to 1:30 at Mayler's Café in LocalCity. The cost of the luncheon is $20 and reservations can be made at www.LocalCityCoC.com.

Smith's 'Career Pivot' presentation is the latest offering in the Chamber's ongoing Lunch-and-Learn Program featuring topics of value to LocalCity's businesses and residents. With so many diverse new businesses opening in LocalCity, Smith's topic proves especially timely. "The vibrancy of LocalCity's business environment creates all kinds of opportunities," Smith says, adding: "A perfect new career might be waiting right here in LocalCity – with a higher salary, easier commute and far better work-life balance. You just have to know how to look beyond job titles and business categories to recognize them."

About GoalCoach, LLC: Founded by Certified Life Coach Chris Smith, GoalCoach helps people build self-awareness, define priorities and set a series of small goals that open the way to dramatic achievements and deep satisfaction. For a free introductory coaching session, contact Chris Smith at Chris@GoalCoach.com or 123-444-5678.

--END--

SECTION 3:
ENGAGEMENT

Now that you have your basic toolkit, the next goal is to engage the attention of new prospects and motivate them to call and schedule a coaching session. You also need to retain your visibility and value with existing and former clients.

In this section, we're going to look at how to create engagement using tools like pricing, packaging, giveaways and guarantees. But first, we're going to create your value proposition because that's going to shape *the specific kind of offers, materials and tactics* best suited for ***your*** different audiences.

CREATING THE RIGHT VALUE PROPOSITION

A value proposition is 'what's in it' for your client. Think about your specific target audience. Who are they? What types of goals do they want to reach? What is the benefit they'll receive from reaching these goals? In other words, what kinds of rewards will they experience in their lives? For example: A *goal* may be losing 20 pounds, but the *reward* may be feeling more attractive and having more energy.

Think about ***one*** of your target audiences. List the specific goals/benefits that motivate them:

My Target Audience Is:	Typical Goals Are:	Rewards of Reaching These Goals:

Now, let's turn these motivators into a value proposition. Do it by adding your personal branding. Think back to the '*BECAUSE*' exercise in the PERSONAL BRANDING section. Using the same process, let's pair your brand (who you are and how you approach things) with a reward your audience values.

Because I: (brand trait)	You: (goal + reward)
Example: Because I help you work with strengths you already have ...	... you can move forward *faster*, not just losing weight, but also *feeling* lighter – more confident, energized and powerful.

By linking your brand traits and differentiators to the rewards that motivate your audience, you create a compelling value proposition. You'll use this value proposition on your website, in your brochure and in networking conversations.

USING OFFERS TO REMOVE 'STOPPERS'

Going through the goal/reward process helps you create a value proposition that is virtually irresistible to your target audience. *Virtually* – because they may fear something that outweighs your value proposition. For example:

- "I'm afraid that even with a life coach I will fail to achieve my goal."
- "This is going to be so expensive."
- "Time! How LONG would it take to see a difference?"

For prospects to engage with your value proposition, you've got to get them over these 'stoppers'. Your Basic Toolkit will help, but a good offer makes the difference.

An offer is made up of four components: *value proposition, pricing, packaging* and a *guarantee*.

Before we look closer at all four components, let's focus for just a moment on how to set your life coaching fees.

Setting Your Life Coaching Fees

First, *HOW* you will charge:

Some coaches charge by the session. This is fine, but it *does* create challenges. For instance, if you charge by the session, you may have to work harder for your clients to appreciate that *several* sessions are typical or even that coaching can be an ongoing relationship over the years.

This is why some coaches prefer to charge *by the month* instead of by the session. They're quoting potential clients a bigger price, but immediately showing that it's broken down over multiple sessions as a regular recurring investment (like a club membership or clothing allowance).

Next, *WHAT* you will charge:

Your fee depends on your experience, niche and certifications. Pricing also varies in different parts of the country. Googling life coaches in your area will help you get a feel for your own specific market.

To give you a ballpark for pricing, new coaches typically charge in the $50-$75 range per session ($200-300 per month), with highly experienced executive coaches charging upwards of $500 for a monthly session.

VALUE PROPOSITION + PRICING + PACKAGING + GUARANTEE = OFFER

Together, these four elements create an offer that outweighs the stoppers so your value proposition tips the scale in favor of signing up for coaching sessions. Once you define your value proposition, you'll want to add the right pricing, packaging and guarantee for each audience. Below are a few ideas to get you started:

PRICING	PACKAGING	GUARANTEE
First coaching session free Preferred rate (for returning clients) Seasonal pricing (e.g. New Year's Resolution, high school or college graduation) Birthday Coaching Session: Your Discount = Your Age Pay in installments (for a seminar, for instance)	Purchase a 4-session package and get your 4th session free Purchase a 4-session package by [date] and save 25% Register for my new 3-Session Program on [topic] Attend my seminar and receive your first private coaching session free	If you're not completely satisfied with the value of your first coaching session, pay nothing. (NOTE: what you're agreeing to give away is the initial session, which most coaches already offer free of charge.) You'll leave each session understanding specific steps you can take toward achieving your goal – or your money back.

Here's an example of a complete offer statement using a weight-loss goal. Note how the statement addresses the ***STOPPERS***:

> I'll help you work with ***strengths you already have*** so you can move forward faster. Best of all, coaching will help you do more than lose weight: you'll begin to feel lighter – more confident, energized and powerful. ***And it won't take forever!*** I offer a 4-session package ***proven to accelerate weight loss***. Sign up for the program and save ***25% off*** the regular per-session rate. Plus, if you're not satisfied with the value of your first session, I'll ***refund*** the price you paid for the full program, including that first session.

You'll need more than one offer. As you start your practice, you may want to experiment with different audiences to find your niche. As you build your practice, you'll need offers that motivate current coaching clients to continue on with you for additional sessions. You'll also need to design offers to bring former clients back on board for a new seminar or fresh series of coaching sessions.

CREATING EFFECTIVE GIVEAWAYS

Giveaways can be an excellent tool for engaging your audiences. They keep you visible and top of mind. Use giveaways to educate your audiences about coaching and your own brand of coaching. Giveaways invite interaction, and the more you and your audiences interact, the more the stoppers fall away.

The secret, however, is not to settle for any old giveaway. Instead, find something that is uniquely yours and specifically related to coaching. Below is a brainstorm-starter list of possible giveaways:

THE GIVEAWAY	THE SECRET
A short report, guide or eBook you've written (topics might include stress, caregiving, burnout, healthy choices, boundaries ...)	Give away 90% of the solution to a specific challenge. Describe how the rest of the solution depends on the unique person and situation and how a few coaching sessions can reveal this solution.
An inexpensive planner	Tuck in a hand-written note about how quickly goals can be met when we become intentional. End with an open-ended question, like: "Where would you like to be three months from now?" (And, three months ahead – actually write a note in the planner: "Imagine what's possible!")
A XX-Day Action Plan	This is a valuable giveaway because it reinforces the strategies and steps you've explored during coaching. Putting a set timeframe on it gives you a reason to check back with clients, and that gives them the chance to say: "I need your help!"
A tool – like a Life Wheel – for assessing where issues are arising	Use a Life Wheel that reflects your own unique niche and approach to coaching. *Make sure you put your name and contact information on it.*

Perfect occasions for using giveaways:

- At the end of a seminar, first coaching session, or the end of a series of sessions
- 3 months after a client has had a final session
- Beginning/end of the year
- A client or former client's birthday
- Offering them on your Facebook page
- Handing them out at events and speaking engagements

ENGAGING CURRENT AND PAST CLIENTS

Your current and former clients are prime prospects for new coaching sessions, seminars and other offerings. In the NETWORKING section, we'll look at how to approach these clients to ask for referrals and new business. Right now, however, let's look at ways to keep these important people engaged so when the time comes to promote a seminar or refer business, they're very much in touch with you and your practice.

For starters, maintain an up-to-date file of your clients. This can be a simple table in Word, an Excel spreadsheet or – if you're app-savvy and growing a large client base – a contact database. Consider using these fields:

Name	Address	Email and phone	Date started with me	Coaching topics	Birthday	Sessions attended/last session
Casper, Amy	123 Hill Rd., Jones MD 20914	ACasper@gmail.com 555-123-4567	5/2016	Work-life balance, confidence	JUN xx, 1978	Private sessions x 6 Confidence Seminar Last: 1/2017

Creating regular 'touches' with your clients

Using your contact file, you can set up a simple but effective Customer Relationship Management program. For instance, each month you might search on the **Date started with me** field of the file to call up the coming month's 'anniversaries' and send a quick card or email to clients.

For example:

> X (years/months) ago, we were having our first coaching session! Time goes so quickly, doesn't it? When you have a moment, I'd love to hear how things are going.
>
> Using the last **Sessions attended/last session** field, you can check back with clients or prospects to whom you've given action plans. You can also suggest new sessions: "Since we worked together on X, I've developed a new 2-session program on Y you might find valuable ..."

Section 3: Engagement

There are so many opportunities for staying in touch! You'll find more ideas in the NETWORKING and SOCIAL MEDIA sections. But in terms of actual engagement, here are the three 'touches' to make sure you send throughout the year:

1. **End of year/new year message.** This is a critical time for coaches to be visible.

2. **April/May update on what's happening in your practice –** growth, new offerings, observations.

3. **August/September check in.** You might say something like this: "Often, summer gives us time to think about changes we'd like to make. If there's a change or goal you have in mind, let's see if we can achieve it by the end of the year!"

SECTION 4:
NETWORKING

BEST TYPES OF NETWORKING FOR LIFE COACHES

Three types of networking are most effective for promoting visibility as a life coach: professional networking clubs, community organizations and casual networking. Let's look at each of these opportunities.

Professional Networking Clubs

These are groups where members get together expressly for the purpose of generating leads for each other. Typically, these groups limit who can join so there are no conflicts of interest. For example, you might find yourself in a group with a real estate agent, CPA, chiropractor, computer consultant, and a variety of small business owners, but you would be the only life coach. These groups tend to meet frequently (weekly) and members are expected to arrive at each meeting ready to report on their success in referring business to the other members of the group.

Networking clubs can be an extremely effective way to build loyal referrers who help you grow your coaching practice. It will, however, take a lot of commitment to make each meeting. Plus, unless you have a substantial group of friends and contacts, it could be difficult to generate leads for the other members of the group. But if you do bump into lots of people and have time for a weekly breakfast or lunch, this could be absolutely ideal for you.

Examples of Professional Networking Clubs

- BNI (Business Networking International)
- WIB (Women in Business)
- Professional Networking Meetups (www.MeetUp.com)

Community Organizations

The more visible you are in your community, the more people learn to associate you with life coaching and begin to refer people to you ... and even call you themselves. Community groups – including those to which you already belong – may be a perfect way to build your practice.

Again, though, it takes commitment. You won't enjoy much visibility unless you stay active: attend meetings, participate in events, volunteer, even take on speaking engagements. Since these groups are focused on a cause rather than on networking, expect your recognition *and your referrals* to build more slowly than with networking clubs. Still, once you begin to build momentum, these organizations can reward you with a steady flow of new coaching clients.

Examples of Community Organizations

- Chamber of Commerce
- Rotary, Lions, Kiwanis, Optimists, etc.
- Home Owners Association
- School Groups (PTA, sports Booster Club, etc.)

Casual Networking

Casual networking is the practice of promoting your visibility as a coach as you go about your ordinary day. You do this simply by being friendly and interested in what others are saying – skills that are typically strong in life coaches!

Casual networking is an essential skill to hone, and one that can be used even if joining groups is outside your comfort zone.

Examples of Opportunities for Casual Networking

- The gym
- Clubs (tennis, cards, wine, books, etc.)
- Hair salon
- Parties
- Children's team practices
- Meetup groups for special interests (running, hiking, women's interests, etc. – find them and sign up at www.MeetUp.com)

EXERCISE: Targeting Your Best Networking Opportunities

1. **Using the list below as a starting point,** brainstorm the clubs, organizations or casual types of networking that appeal to you. At this point, don't worry about time commitments, just pick 3 that seem like a good fit for your interests and comfort zone.

NETWORKING CLUB	COMMUNITY GROUPS	CASUAL NETWORKING
BNI WIB Networking Meetups Local groups (Google 'Join networking group')	School Civic Groups Chamber of Commerce Homeowners Association Church/Religious Groups	Clubs Gym Spa or Salon Friends Family Sports practices/events

Possible opportunity #1: ______________________

Possible opportunity #2: ______________________

Possible opportunity #3: ______________________

2. **For the three opportunities, define the potential clients/referrers in each group.** We've filled in an example. Remember, the simple act of brainstorming can yield good ideas about how to promote coaching-specific services that will be of most value to each audience.

OPPORTUNITY	PROSPECTS/REFERRERS	HOW CAN I HELP THEM?
High School Booster Club	Single moms/dads & Couples age 40s/50s Probably working	Stress/weight management Starting fresh when kids graduate Getting control: money/life

3. **How much time can you reasonably invest in networking?** _____________ hours per week

4. **Now, look at the opportunities you've identified.** How well does the time commitment for these opportunities match up with your bandwidth? Is there an expense involved (e.g., membership fee, cost of weekly or monthly luncheon, etc.). How quickly could you expect to begin seeing referrals? Once the momentum picks up, how many clients do you think you could reasonably expect to develop from each opportunity? Note that if the activity is something you're already doing (like going to a gym or attending sports practices, list the cost and hours as zero).

OPPORTUNITY	HOURS	FEES/COST	HOW LONG?	POTENTIAL ROI
High School Booster Club	(2) 1-hour meetings + work snack stand 1 game per season	A donation toward the club is probably expected	0-3 months	2-3 clients per sports season

5. **At this point you may see a perfect match.** Or, you might see that while a professional networking club could be your best bet to ramp up referrals quickly, you just can't commit to weekly meetings. So look back to less demanding networking opportunities like monthly Chamber of Commerce luncheons or one-time events (like running your school's silent auction fundraiser). Or, you may see that the time and money for any of the opportunities you identified is simply too much for the ROI you can reasonably expect. If that's the case, put your time and budget toward tactics that align better for you, like social media.

TIPS FOR STARTING CONVERSATIONS AND WORKING A CROWD

Instead of feeling you must sell your services, simply look for genuine opportunities to help.

For example: Imagine you're at your health club walking on the treadmill. Since the pace is easy and there's a social culture at your club, you're having a light conversation with someone walking on the treadmill next to you. While the two of you have spoken casually before, those conversations have never gone into what he does or what you do. Then, he mentions something about how hard it is for him to get to the gym because his work schedule is so intense. This presents an opportunity for you to help.

You might start by saying something to validate his challenge: *"It is hard to balance an intense work schedule with getting to the gym."* Then, you could add something like, *"You know, I'm a life coach, and finding ways to carve out more personal time is one of the most common goals my clients want to reach."* And then, so you don't sound too salesy, turn the conversation back to him with a question, something like: *"You're here despite your intense schedule. What do you think the secret is?"*

This might open up a discussion about what you do as a life coach, giving you the opportunity to offer a free coaching session. Or, the conversation might drift in another direction. That's fine – at least he knows you're a life coach.

HOW TO PREPARE

- **Know something new.** If you're going to a Chamber of Commerce event, for example, look for local news (like housing trends), business trends, or information about a new business opening in town. For 'gym talk,' keep an eye out for new fitness tips. Scan Google news, the Huffington Post, etc. and roll through the headlines to find general news that you might use as a springboard for conversations.

- **Plan what you might say next.** Looking at the news you've gathered (above), think of how you might use the news as an opportunity to talk about life coaching. For example, you might find a news item about a new business in town that's been started by a couple who have switched careers and are following a passion or trying something totally new. Think of how you might use that as an opening to extend the conversation: "What passion would you follow?" might be the perfect way to start a discussion about how setting small goals can make big changes possible – and before you know it, you're talking about your own passion for helping other people make changes and achieve dreams.

HOW TO INTRODUCE YOURSELF

Use the 10-second elevator pitch you created in the BASIC TOOLKIT section. With professional networking clubs, you're typically given 45-seconds to introduce yourself. You can just expand your regular elevator pitch, but doing the same introduction every week throws away opportunities to show different aspects of yourself and your life coaching practice. Here are a few ways to switch up the additional 35 seconds you have:

- Tell something interesting you've just helped a client achieve
- Share the top 3 reasons clients are coming to you
- Share that you've just coached your 50th client or hit your 100th coaching session
- Give quick examples:
  - How to set a goal
  - The question behind the question (don't ask who, ask what)
  - How changing your outlook changes the outcome
  - How to get unstuck
- Explain a coaching concept:
  - Emotional Intelligence
  - Neurolinguistic Programming (NLP)
  - Power poses
  - SMART goals

HOW TO CONNECT

- **Project relaxed confidence.** Even if you feel nervous, consciously open your body posture and relax. Meet people's glances with a smile and nod. This all conveys that you're approachable and easy to talk to.

- **Look for a way to join in.** Look for people standing alone or groups standing in an open U-shape (vs. four people forming a circle). Don't try to join a group that physically looks closed or where two or more people are talking intently. Even if they welcome you, they'll quickly return to what they were discussing and you'll feel awkward.

- **Listen for a way to join in.** If the conversation is light and someone makes a humorous statement, the simple act of laughing can be enough to make you part of the group.

  You can also listen for a chance to join in the conversation, but don't interrupt. Wait for a natural pause. Then, you might ask a question about something that was said or pick up on a point that was made. Or, if that line of conversation has pretty much played out, you can relaunch the conversation using one of the news items that you prepared in advance. You can make the transition to the new topic by saying something like, "Hey, I [heard, saw, learned] something the other day that might interest you all [and proceed with your news item]."

HOW TO ENGAGE

- **Keep it light.** You simply want to make an initial connection. So start with a simple, "Hello," and keep your tone light and positive.

- **Start the ball rolling.** The goal here is just to start a conversation and then do what life coaches naturally do best: ask good questions and listen!

  One-on-one or in a group with people you know, a great starter question is, "What are you up to these days?" That might be enough to kickstart an entire conversation. Just be ready! If someone replies, "Not much. What about you?" be prepared to say something like, "I'm loving my work! Lately, I've been using the same goal-setting techniques I use with clients to [name a small goal]. It really is amazing – once you can get clear about what changes you want to make, the steps for getting there seem surprisingly simple."

  From there you can engage others. For example: "Is there something you've wanted to do that just isn't getting done?" And you're off and running in a lively conversation that is engaging, thought-provoking and energizing for everyone.

  With a group you don't know, you can always ask, "How do you know each other?" (Or, at parties, "How do you know the host?"). You can comment on the news, the food, or even the weather – but add a conversation 'peg' that helps the other person think of something to say. Here's an example:

  > *"It's so cold today! But everyone has still come out for the luncheon. Where I grew up, we'd be* ***hibernating*** *at these temperatures."*

  This makes you so much fun to talk to because the other person isn't stuck for conversation. He can easily respond, "Where did you grow up?" and even follow on with "How did you end up here?" and sooner or later you're going to be in a free-flowing conversation and there will be natural opportunities to talk about your life coaching practice.

- **Stay on brand.** Make sure the things you talk about and the way you talk about them reflect your brand themes. Also, talk about your practice the way you *want* it to be. Even if you have only a few clients, talk about the importance of your work, the difference it makes in lives and all the ways you can help people achieve goals.

  To be clear: don't misrepresent your practice, just don't downsize the importance of your skills and expertise.

  This gives you an air of authority which inspires trust – and new business referrals. It also makes you memorable. Both of these goals are exactly what your networking *should* accomplish.

WHERE TO LOOK FOR OPPORTUNITIES

One of the best ways to spot opportunities for life coaching is to look for them. Here is a quick list designed to spark your own thinking as you look around at your friends, colleagues, and community.

OPPORTUNITIES TO HELP PEOPLE MAKE TRANSITIONS

- High school to college
- College to career
- Old career to new career
- Old job to new job
- Returning to work after a gap
- Empty nest
- Relocation
- Retirement

OPPORTUNITIES TO HELP PEOPLE GROW

- Professional growth or performance
- Set and achieve personal goals
- Find more purpose/passion in life
- Be more at ease socially/professionally
- Make healthy lifestyle changes
- Increase energy and motivation
- Develop a new level of spirituality
- Get better control over the quantity and quality of family time
- Follow through on a budget or financial plan

OPPORTUNITIES TO HELP PEOPLE COPE WITH CHALLENGES

- Becoming a caretaker for a loved one
- Divorce
- Loss of a loved one
- Dealing with difficult bosses/co-workers
- Relationships
- Parenting
- Getting 'unstuck'
- Self-esteem

Just reading through this list you can probably think of dozens more opportunities. And that's the point! By focusing attention on where opportunities might exist, you'll find these opportunities start to unfold as if by magic.

WAYS TO USE BUSINESS CARDS EFFECTIVELY

Presenting Your Card

- **Keep it fresh.** A faded, dog-eared business card tells a hundred stories about you and your life coaching practice – none of them good. It's okay to pull out a few cards to keep handy in your pocket at a networking event, but otherwise keep your cards in a case to protect them.
- **Don't be in a hurry.** Try to wait until the other person asks for your card. Or wait until the conversation is winding down to offer your card.
- **Ask, "May I give you my card?"** It's polite and it makes the process of exchanging cards more personal and memorable. This gives your card more perceived value.
- **Don't give multiple cards** unless you're asked for them. Doing so implies that even though you've just met, you're expecting the other person to put her reputation on the line and pass out your cards. That's extremely off-brand because building trust and credibility is such a critical part of life coaching.

Receiving Business Cards

- **Always look at the card you're given –** never just slip it into your purse or pocket.
- **Comment on the card:** "What a beautiful card!" or "Oh, your office is in the historic part of downtown, isn't it?" etc.
- **Thank the person.** Treat the card as if you're truly glad to have it – *and* to have met the person: "Thank you! I really enjoyed meeting you. I do hope we'll be in touch."

Other Ways To Use Business Cards

There are all kinds of crazy 'guerilla' tactics for using business cards, like leaving them on the windshields of parked cars or leaving one on the restaurant table with the tip. Tactics like these are so wrong for life coaches! Your brand is about confidentiality, respect and making a highly valuable personal connection with your clients. Printing a thousand cheap business cards and leaving them everywhere undercuts every aspect of that brand. There are, however, ways to use business cards that do make sense for life coaches:

- **Referrers:** You may find that non-competing businesses may be happy to have a small supply of your business cards on hand. We'll talk more about referrers in the following pages.
- **Community Bulletin Boards:** Often, it can be quite effective to pin your card to a bulletin board if it's in the right place. Just make sure that the board gives you visibility to the audience you want as clients. Upscale grocery stores, coops, retirement communities, local cafés, gyms, spas, libraries and other locations can give you good visibility.
- **Business Card Ads:** Your business card can become a ready-to-use ad in church bulletins, school yearbooks, community resource guides, conference programs, HOA newsletters and similar venues. It doesn't just have to be a print ad – many hyper-local news sites are cropping up (like 'Patch' services that provide news for a particular town) and you can run your business card as a banner ad – simple and easy.

HOW TO ASK FOR REFERRALS

Asking clients, friends and even new contacts for referrals can become very easy. It can also become one of the most effective ways to grow your practice. If you're not a natural networker, however, you may benefit from a little coaching. Simply use the examples below as your starting point for finding your own comfort-zone approach in asking for referrals.

MINDSET: Asking for a referral is not asking for a favor.

You are asking for the opportunity to help people.

Example of Asking for a Referral

"I really enjoyed working with you! I'm so inspired by what you've achieved and honored to have been part of your journey. It's why I became a life coach. If there is anything else I can help with, please let me know. And if you know of anyone else who might benefit from coaching, I'd welcome a referral, especially from you. Just tell them to mention you and I'll provide their introductory session free."

Always say "Thank You" for a referral. Even if someone has referred clients to you a dozen times, still take the time to thank them. An email or call is fine, but follow up with a small gift – a gift card for Starbucks®, Amazon® or iTunes® are great ideas and they're easy to send via email or to tuck in an envelope with a thank you note.

Example of Asking a Non-client for a Referral

"You know, for so many people, even a few life coaching sessions can make all the difference. If you know of anyone looking to make a fresh start, figure things out or get more control over their lives at work or home, I would love to see what we could accomplish – even in just one session. In fact, if you do know someone, have them contact me and mention your name – I'll give them the first session for free."

Variation for using this approach as a follow-up note after talking with someone:

"I really enjoyed talking with you today. It's so true how crazy things get with work and life. I see it all the time in my practice. I also see that even a few life coaching sessions can make a difference. In fact, even *one* session can make a difference. If you know anyone who is struggling with work/life balance or how to make a fresh start with a career, relationships or lifestyle, I would love to offer them a free session. Just have them contact me and mention your name. In the meantime, enjoy [that new car]! Hope to see you again soon."

How to Find Referral Partners

Referral partners are the informal version of professional networking clubs. These are people in businesses that don't compete with your life coaching practice and that have clients who might value your services. In exchange for referring clients, these partners would value referrals from you for their businesses. The referral-partner relationship can be as simple as a gym letting you leave a stack of business cards by the front desk, or as robust as joining with a personal trainer to offer 'mind/body' packages.

Here are a few ideas to get you thinking about possible referral partners.

Potential Referral Partners	A Few Reasons They Might Refer You
School counselors, tutors, educational consultants	• Help students with self-confidence • Help parents with work/life balance • Help students transition from high school to college • Help graduates transition into careers
Doctors, chiropractors, nurses	• Help patients make lifestyle changes for better health • Help caregivers balance demands/deal with stress • Help with fresh starts for people going through divorce, loss of a loved one, life transition
OB-GYNs	• Help moms with work/life balance • Help set goals for losing 'baby weight' • Help moms transition to a more baby-friendly job
Nursing homes	• Help loved ones 'sandwiched' by family needs • Help caregivers with self-care goals
Active retirement communities	• Help newly retired people find/follow their purpose • Help survivors make a fresh start after losing a loved one
Personal trainer	• Help people with work/life balance • Help people grow in their careers • Help people develop new confidence and self-esteem to go with their new physical strength
Business owners, HR people and employee assistance programs	• Help employees learn how to get things done • Help employees define goals for development • Support culture change: promoting accountability, ending toxic chatter, etc.

A Word About Referral Services

The ICF (International Coach Federation) tends to be the gold standard for referring life coaches. But if you're not an ICF-certified coach, this isn't a referral source that's open to you. Some life coaches have found it worthwhile to invest in one of the online life coach referral services. Two that get mentioned a lot are Noomii ($400/year to join and you get a money-back guarantee) and Christian Coaches (about $100/year).

USING ARTICLES TO NURTURE LEADS

As a rule of thumb, it takes seven 'touches' to convert a contact or lead into a client. One of the easiest ways to stay in touch is by sharing helpful information. In the next section (Social Media) we'll talk about how to do this on sites like LinkedIn and Facebook. Here, let's focus on how to use articles.

What kind of articles will work best for nurturing life-coaching leads?

- Articles that are relevant to where you met (e.g., Chamber of Commerce, school, etc.)
- Articles about interests your contact or lead has expressed (starting a new business, retirement, being more productive at work, etc.)
- Articles about life coaching

Where do you find these articles?

- **Search the web:** For example, if someone mentioned going on a much-anticipated vacation, Google the name of the destination or packing tips.
- **Keep a 'To Share' file:** As you come across interesting tidbits (print or online), add them to a file you keep on your computer. You can cut and paste URLs or scan print pieces so they're ready to copy or use with emails.
- **Credible life coaching sources:** Check out sites like the ICF, IAC (International Association of Coaching), etc.

NEVER present these materials as your own work. ALWAYS give the credits for where you found materials.

You can also find ready-to-use articles on coaching at The LiveWell Institute, including:

- What is Life Coaching?
- What is the ROI of Life Coaching?
- Facts and Myths About Life Coaching
- Life Coach Case Studies
- And more

These articles can be a good way to introduce prospects to life coaching and the value it offers.

www.TheLiveWellInstitute.com

How do you use the articles?

- Attachments or URLs sent with emails
- Sent with a note
- Given to contacts the next time you see them
- Given out at events where you make a presentation (with your card stapled to them)
- Given to referral partners, etc.

SECTION 5:
SOCIAL MEDIA

WHY SOCIAL MEDIA IS PERFECT FOR LIFE COACHES

Social media gives you a platform for promoting your practice in so many ways! It's networking, referrals, engagement, credibility, brand-building, public relations and information-sharing all rolled into one. Best of all, the interactive nature of social media gives you a way to use comfort zone strengths that define life coaches: the ability to listen, ask good questions and engage with people.

Before looking at your own social media presence, let's look at what's possible. Here's a snapshot of how an actual coach used Facebook to grow an audience of 1,400 Friends – and a full schedule of clients.

Case Study: Growing a Coaching Practice Through Facebook

For several years, 'Rhonda' eked out a small coaching income. It was hard to find clients. Once she helped clients through a specific issue, they moved on. She had to keep replacing them.

STEP 1: GETTING VISIBLE. At a networking event, Rhonda met a consultant who regularly hosted free lead-generating teleseminars for women business owners. The Consultant asked Rhonda to participate as a guest speaker. Rhonda prepared a short presentation on how coaching can help entrepreneurs look and feel more confident, and the value that adds to a business. As part of her presentation, Rhonda said she would be posting more about coaching and confidence on her Facebook Group and she invited participants to visit and join her group.

STEP 2: BONDING. As teleconference participants joined, Rhonda's group grew to 59 people in three days. Each time a new member joined, Rhonda welcomed them. Her posts – which were visible to the entire group – were simple: "Hi, Mary! Welcome to our coaching group. Tell us a little about yourself." As conversations developed between members, Rhonda gained key insights into her audience. She used these insights to shape the tips she was posting about how to develop and project confidence.

STEP 3: GROWING. After a month, Rhonda's group had grown to 200 members, 6 of whom became new clients interested in developing their sense of confidence. Rhonda began to expand from posts on confidence to other coaching topics. Instead of leaving once they had achieved some goals around confidence, clients stayed. They continued working with Rhonda on a regular basis to achieve additional goals. They shared their progress with the Facebook group. Within 6 months, Rhonda's group had over 1,400 members.

STEP 4: TAILORING. Rhonda's coaching schedule was filling up. Without being able to add more hours to her week, Rhonda looked at ways to increase her hourly rate. To do this, she created a 5-session coaching 'intensive' designed to help women business owners create a clear vision for their company and set specific steps and goals for achieving that vision. Instead of charging her per-session rate, she doubled that rate and charged a single flat rate for the program. Not only did a significant number of women sign on for the intensive, they stayed on board afterward for monthly coaching at that same higher rate.

Note that this entire Facebook program cost Rhonda $0. Clearly we see social media's potential!

SETTING UP YOUR SOCIAL MEDIA PAGES

Facebook

Facebook Pages let you set up a page for your business. You can include your business profile and share photos, links, videos and posts the same way you do on your personal Facebook page. Invite friends and colleagues to become fans and share just as they would on a personal page. Once they become fans and follow you, they automatically see your posts and posts of other fans.

Facebook Groups let you set up additional pages for particular groups. For instance, if you deal with different types of life coaching clients, you might want to set up a group page to focus the discussion and content on specific areas of interest to each group. Your group participants are members, not fans, so the sharing is visible only to group members rather than on Facebook home feeds.

Apps. Facebook is always coming out with new tools for giving your posts greater visibility. You can have ads appear to users with certain demographics or who click on certain types of content. You can pay to have your posts 'boosted' so they don't get buried among other postings. The best place to learn about these apps is directly from Facebook:

For how-to help with pages, groups and apps:
www.facebook.com/business/

LinkedIn

Your Profile. This isn't a job description, it's a personal profile of you. Be clear, concise, and true to your brand. Include who you are, how you're different, and why that difference matters to *others*. When someone reads your profile, they should have a sense of your personality (word choices), your expertise (certifications) and, most important, how you can help them.

Your Business Profile. Like Facebook, LinkedIn allows you to set up a page for yourself and one for your business.

Groups. Whether you create a group or join one, take the commitment seriously and be active in posting and commenting.

Recommendations. The way to get recommendations is to give them. Be a good LinkedIn 'citizen' – go through your list of contacts and recommend them for specific skills. You'll find that people repay the favor and recommend *you*.

YouTube

Your YouTube Channel. A YouTube channel is like a Facebook or LikedIn page but you post videos. With the right keywords, your videos may attract a large following. You can also post videos on your YouTube Channel and then link to them from your website – a very easy way to post videos! To learn how to create your YouTube Channel, go to: **www.youtube.com/create_channel**

WHERE DO YOU FIND *YOUR* AUDIENCE?

Of the roughly 7 billion people on the planet, about 3 billion are engaged with social media. The better you harness the reach and visibility possible through social media, the faster you can grow your life coaching practice. So where do you start? The popularity of sites changes and so do the number of people using those sites. But for now at least, it's a good bet that life coaches can find their audience on these main social media platforms:

- **Facebook.** Ninety percent of people who go online use Facebook. Facebook is a great place to gain visibility as a life coach because it's a *conversational* site where people discuss all kinds of situations coming up in their lives. You can use both your personal Facebook page and a Facebook page for your practice to enter into these conversations.
- **LinkedIn.** A lot of people think of LinkedIn as just a resumé site. Used well, LinkedIn is far more. It gives you the opportunity to engage in groups on topics that are relevant to your life coaching practice. Like the networking opportunities we looked at earlier, LinkedIn can bring you together with others in ways that are not directly related to life coaching, but that build your visibility *as a life coach.* Again, you may want both a personal profile and one of your life coaching practice.
- **YouTube.** What kind of video would a life coach post on YouTube? Helpful ones that explain what life coaching is, give tips and even present mini case studies. Once you post your video on YouTube, you can link to it in emails, Facebook, LinkedIn and from your website.

> People who use social media use multiple sites. But they don't use multiple sites *equally*: 91% of people who use Twitter also use Facebook. 84% of people who use LinkedIn also use Facebook. But of the people who use Facebook, only 29% also use Twitter and only 33% also use LinkedIn.

- **Blogging.** Many coaches have built large followings for their own blogs. To do this, you must be committed to posting content that is *original, useful,* and *regular*. Opinions have far less value than real-world examples, tips, etc. If you are considering a blog, be realistic about the amount of content you can generate and time you can commit because if you *don't* keep up, your audience falls away and your out-of-date blog brands you as someone who doesn't follow through.

If you have *limited* bandwidth: focus on Facebook and LinkedIn. YouTube doesn't demand such a consistent supply of content, so almost everyone has time to create and post short videos.

If you have a *little more* bandwidth: include Twitter and (if your target audience is female) Pinterest. Pinterest is visual, so you'll need to create photos with inspirational messages or helpful, how-to tips on goal setting, getting unstuck, etc. We'll explain quick and easy ways to do this in the following pages.

If you have *a lot* of bandwidth: include a blog.

WHAT TO POST?

As a coach, your topic is *life:* strategies for coping with ups and downs, how to achieve balance, move forward, realize dreams – the list is virtually endless. But often, that's the problem. Life coaching is such a broad category that it can be difficult to figure out how to focus on the content that's most relevant for your own brand and your own life coaching practice.

The secret to creating social media posts that actually engage your audience is this: give away 99% of a concept, but retain 1% of the concept (tip, method, etc.) that makes the solution possible.

Remember: the purpose of posting is not just to be visible. The purpose is to get visible so that people relate to you and realize their own opportunities for benefiting from your life coaching services.

Here are a few categories to help you begin to brainstorm.

Type of Posting	Examples
TIPS	
• How to say no by	saying yes • Ways to create more space in your day • Smarter ways to set SMART goals • 3 positive coping techniques
QUESTIONS	• What's stopping you? • Why do we stay stuck? • How do you define confidence? • What isn't working for you any more? • Can you avoid negative self-messages for one day?
OBSERVATIONS	• More people are looking for greater meaning • Observe how you react when you're criticized • Be aware of your most productive times of day • Personal observations: What I find works for me
TRANSFORMATIONS	• The first step of getting 'unstuck' is to know what you *do* want vs. what you *don't* want any more • What would a new life look like for you? • How would it feel to ...
SURPRISES	• The best way to make big changes is to make little ones • What is a goal? (it's not what you think) • Your comfort zone might be a good place • Changing how you walk can change how you feel

TIP: If you share something socially, **monitor the activity for 48 to 72 hours and engage** with the responders. Simply saying "Thank you" for liking, sharing or retweeting creates a bond between you and the people engaging with your content.

HOW TO ADAPT POSTINGS FOR DIFFERENT SITES

Different social media sites have different spins on content. Chances are you've seen the famous photo of a whiteboard (originally posted by Douglas Wray on Instagram in 2012) that uses donuts to explain social media. Here's an excerpt of what's written on the whiteboard in that photo:

Twitter	I'm eating a donut
Facebook	I like donuts
YouTube	Here I am eating a donut
LinkedIn	My skills include donut eating
Pinterest	Here's a donut recipe

So how do we translate this for life coaching? Here's an example of how to use the donut concept to adapt the same content for different social media:

Twitter	I'm giving myself new messages about myself
Facebook	I like how the small step of changing what I say about myself is changing how I feel about myself
YouTube	Here I am demonstrating how I'm replacing old messages about myself with new ones ("I'm swamped" vs. "My day is very full")
LinkedIn	I help people change the messages they give themselves about what's possible
Pinterest	Here's a 'poster' showing how to replace common negative self-messages with positive ones

Using this basic approach, you see how you can post the SAME content in DIFFERENT ways. That means you don' t need to come up with different ideas for each social media site, you just need to approach that content differently for each.

You need to post *regularly*. You should aim to post at least weekly on Facebook, LinkedIn and Twitter. But before you post, ask yourself these questions:

1. Is this post 'on brand' – does it reflect the right tone, point of view and my life coaching niche?
2. Is this post shareable – is it interesting, helpful or provocative enough to start a conversation?
3. Does this post invite engagement – a comment online or a call to find out more about what you do?

How are you going to come up with enough content to post *weekly?* Start with an editorial plan for the next several months. Later in this section you'll find an exercise that helps you create your own social media content plan and timeline.

HOW TO CREATE CONTENT THAT WORKS FOR *YOU*

Of the four websites we've been looking at, YouTube and Facebook are a life coach's easiest venues. The only secret is creating content that's *original*. Here's why: If all you do is share *others'* tips, inspiration and ideas, your brand becomes a middleman and you lose your value as a resource and as an expert.

So, how do you create original content that gets shared? Here are a few ideas:

IDEA #1: Create sharable posters

Posters that contain inspirational thoughts, tips or challenges are ideal for sharing with your Facebook friends or posting on Pinterest. Your poster may not go *viral,* but a good one can get shared and seen by a huge audience. To benefit from this exposure be sure posters:

(A) are original – something *you've* created not copied, and

(B) include your name, business name and website URL. Here's an example:

Where to find photos?

Take your own and upload them from your phone or camera. Or purchase one from a stock photo source. Providers like Shutterstock, Getty Images, Dreamstime, FotoStock and RF123 offer images for as little as a few dollars, especially since you don't need to buy large versions of the photos since you'll be using them online.

Once you have your photo ...

Copy the photo into your photo-editing app, add the text and save it as a jpg file.

If you don't have a photo app (or don't know how to use it), here's a workaround: open Microsoft PowerPoint® and copy the photo onto a slide. Choose 'Insert Text Box' and drag the box over the photo. Click the background fill to 'No Fill' and choose a font color that contrasts well with the image. When you're done, save the PowerPoint file as a jpg file. You're ready to upload your photo 'poster' to Facebook or Pinterest.

IDEA #2: Start a survey

Surveys are a wonderful way to engage – and dramatically expand – your friends, fans and followers. Survey Monkey is a web service that makes it simple to send out a survey. You can use your email contact list, for example, to ask for people's inputs *and* to ask them to forward the survey to anyone else they think might want to weigh in. Survey Monkey has *also* created apps that make it equally simple to post your survey on Twitter, LinkedIn or Facebook. For more information, Google: *Survey Monkey make your surveys social.*

Can a survey actually go viral? Well, maybe it won't get hundreds of thousands of 'eyeballs', but you can get some surprising exposure! We know of a coach who sent a one-question survey to 100 people on his email contact list and asked them to forward the survey. He received almost 2,000 responses. He sent the survey results to the original 100 people and again asked them to forward the email. He ended up with 22 inquiries about life coaching – including from people who weren't among the original 100 contacts.

What should you survey?

You can use the editorial content planner that follows to brainstorm topics. Or you can ask for inputs on broad coaching issues and let respondents pick from a list of options. For example: *What is your biggest challenge in trying to balance work and your personal life?*

IDEA #3: Create a video

YouTube is the ideal place for life coaches to post how-to videos. Start with a topic you can address quickly – like how to set a goal, how to appear more confident, the first step in getting 'unstuck,' three things to know about healthy boundaries, etc. For ideas use the editorial content planner that follows. The goal is to pick a topic with wide appeal and provide something quick and easy viewers can do right away to see a difference.

When you're starting out, go short! Plan a video that's about two minutes long. Rehearse until you're comfortable. Make sure your video includes your contact information (you can even just say your website's URL).

How do you create a video?

Someone with a smartphone can record your video for you. Or, you can go to YouTube (where else!!) and view dozens of videos that show you how to use your computer's webcam to create and upload a video of yourself. If you don't want to film yourself talking, you can use PowerPoint® to create a slideshow, record a voice-over, animate the slideshow and upload *that* to YouTube.

No matter how you do the recording, make sure it reflects your personal brand. It's okay if the video doesn't look like a first-run feature film, but *do* experiment with lighting, background and the sound quality to make sure your video comes across as clear, credible and professional.

Also, be sure to post links to your YouTube video on Facebook, LinkedIn and your own website.

EDITORIAL CONTENT PLANNER

1. **Brainstorm broad topics.** Using the ideas below to spark your thinking, come up with 3 broad topics to cover in social media.

Getting unstuck	Life after a loss	Work-life balance	Changing careers
Changing behaviors	Personal productivity	Lifestyle changes	Financial control
Gaining confidence	Decision-making	Setting boundaries	Personal growth

My 1st topic: ______________________________

My 2nd topic: ______________________________

My 3rd topic: ______________________________

2. **Now, list 4 key points you want to make about each topic.** If your topic is about personal productivity, for example, what are 4 ways to improve how you use your time? What are 4 factors that influence personal productivity. Or, what are 4 areas where people struggle, etc.

This creates your 3-month content outline.

MONTHLY TOPICS	WEEKLY TOPICS
First Topic:	1. 2. 3. 4.
Second Topic:	1. 2. 3. 4.
Third Topic:	1. 2. 3. 4.

3. **Now, use the grid below to brainstorm how you'll approach each weekly topic for the social media sites you've targeted.** Refer back to the 'donuts' examples to spin your content for each social media platform.

WEEKLY TOPIC	Facebook	LinkedIn	Twitter
Example: How 'blame' affects personal productivity	Challenge: let's see if we can go a week without blaming someone – share the 'poster' challenge	Tip about the 'Question Behind the Question' – ask what happened, not who did it or why	Statistics on the high cost of blaming others (Did you know ...?)
1.			
2.			
3.			
4.			
1.			
2.			
3.			
4.			
1.			
2.			
3.			
4.			

4. **Now, simply transfer your topics and timing to a calendar.** You'll see exactly when you need to post, what content to cover and where to post it. You can make things even easier by creating chunks of content ahead of time.

BUYING BIGGER EXPOSURE ON SOCIAL MEDIA

There are two types of exposure on social media: organic (the free exposure you get from your friends and group members liking and sharing your posts) and paid. Paid exposure can include search marketing and advertising which we'll cover later. Both Facebook and LinkedIn offer another version of paid exposure – and these could be extremely beneficial for promoting your life coaching practice.

Boosting on Facebook

Facebook gives you the opportunity to 'Boost.' Boosting is a pay-per-view (PPV) advertising tactic that lets you give a post greater visibility. Facebook Boosting tends to be very affordable (at this time, less than $20 for 5,000 views) for exposure with people you otherwise wouldn't reach.

- You can Boost status updates, photos, photo albums, videos and offers.
- Boosted posts come up higher in the News Feed to help more people see them.
- You get exposure to your own Facebook users and additional users who match the geographic and demographic criteria you select.

Whitepaper Campaigns on LinkedIn

From improving personal productivity to finding more effective ways to set boundaries and deal with difficult people, coaches have great stories to tell about transformation. Case studies and coaching tips on a specific topic make for a great whitepaper. You can also use content like this specifically for a LinkedIn Whitepaper Campaign.

- You include a short posting with a snapshot of the whitepaper you've created.
- You give the first page or page and a half.
- The LinkedIn member then provides contact information so you can send the complete report.

HOWEVER: This is *much more expensive* than Facebook Boosting – about $5,000 minimum. If you have a tailored message and a high-ticket coaching offering, this might be worth considering. The $5,000+ barrier to entry keeps the attention high and the quality of whitepapers high, so the exposure can be quite effective.

SECTION 5:
EVENTS

THE VALUE OF HOLDING EVENTS

You became a life coach to help people make positive changes in their lives. You envisioned yourself working one-on-one with clients to achieve goals. But working one-on-one isn't always the fastest way to build your practice, especially when you're getting started. Group events can accelerate your marketing by promoting your practice in several important ways:

- **Visibility:** Your appearance at a group event increases the number of people who know what you do and who may seek your services or recommend you.

- **Credibility:** Serving on panels, speaking at a luncheon, and hosting your own seminar confers expert status. Because of this, people are more likely to trust your skills as a coach. You can leverage this credibility not just with the people who attend the event, but with people who visit your website and see a mention of your recent events and appearances.

- **Education:** While an event may focus on one particular issue (relationships, career development, caregiving, making lifestyle changes, etc.), it also gives you the opportunity to educate the group about what life coaching is and how it works. This makes it easier to market your practice to this group because you can skip the 'how' explanation and focus on your coaching value proposition.

- **Lead generation:** By providing a short intro to a particular topic, your event can start a conversation that invites attendees to follow up with you in personal coaching sessions. Plus, even attendees who don't immediately schedule a session can be included in your spreadsheet of prospects so you can include them in your news, emails and other 'touches' throughout the year.

- **Income:** In addition to speaking engagements and free lead-generation events, coaches can generate income by hosting group events. Consider these sample figures showing potential ROI from the event and the follow-on business:

  1. **Host a 2-hour seminar and charge $75 per person**
     15 people sign up: **$1,125**
  2. **Of those 15 attendees, 2 sign up for coaching**
     2 clients x 4 sessions x $75 .... **$ 600**
  3. **From attendees, you get 1 referral**
     1 client x 4 sessions x $75 .... **$ 300**   **$2,025**
     ($144+/hr)

OPPORTUNITIES FOR EVENTS

Clearly, the ROI of events can be considerable. Below are a few ideas to get you started thinking about the kind of events that interest you and how you can present them or partner in them.

Hosting your own events: Promote them via social media and email using the contact/prospect file you developed in the ENGAGEMENT section.

- **Online webinars/teleconferences.** It's very easy to host an online seminar or a call-in teleconference. If you just want to do the audio conference, there are plenty of conference calling services you can use, many of them free. You'll receive a call-in number and meeting code you can share with people who register. Similarly, videoconferencing services like Webex and Citrix GoToMeeting make it easy to host online webinars. Using the webcam on your computer, laptop or tablet, you can speak to your audience live. Or, simply share a PowerPoint® presentation or photos as you speak. The videoconferencing services provide you with a hyperlink to the screen-sharing session plus a conference call bridge.

- **Onsite events at an organization.** As a benefit to employees or members, many organizations enjoy letting outside experts (like you!) come in and present Lunch-and-Learn sessions. They provide the meeting room, you provide the program.

- **Events at a location you provide.** Libraries, community centers and religious centers often offer meeting rooms that are available free or at a low price. Firms like Regus and hotels also offer business conference rooms and rates can be surprisingly affordable. Note that at venues like these, you may need to bring your own projector to display a PowerPoint® presentation or other computer-based information. You can do your presentation solo or assemble a panel to speak on related topics.

Partnering: Partners will often advertise the event for you. Also use social media and your contact file.

- **Online presentations.** Many Meetup-type organizations like to offer 45-minute online programs to members. You present a 30-minute program and then answer questions. Again, you can use services like Webex or Citrix GoToMeeting to provide visuals while you speak.

- **Doctors, therapists, and other partners.** As noted in the NETWORKING section, coaching is a natural complement to other practices. Local providers may be interested in having you make a presentation as a value-add for their patients. Hospitals, senior-living communities and nursing homes may also be great partners, eager to have a life coach come in and make a presentation to staff, family members and the community.

- **Public speaking.** From PTA evening meetings to Rotary breakfasts and Chamber of Commerce luncheons, organizations are always looking for speakers.

TOPICS FOR PRESENTATIONS

In approaching a partner or doing public speaking, it's good to have a few ready-to-present topics you can offer. What topics? As you define your own personal brand and market niche, you'll find topics that resonate with your audience and that you feel passionate about and confident in presenting.

In the meantime, you can find inspiration from the topics suggested in the SOCIAL MEDIA section.

Here are other strategies for finding the right topic:

1. **Target your topic for a particular organization:** Think about PTA or a doctor's practice – what an organization wants to provide to their members, patients or staff. Then think how coaching can help them deliver.

   For example, a good PTA topic might be *A Coaching Approach to Parenting,* or *Coaching Kids through Homework*. A topic for a doctor's practice might be *Coaching Yourself to Greater Well-Being* or *Coaching Yourself to a Better Night's Sleep*.

2. **Align the topic with your own key differentiators:** In the PERSONAL BRANDING section, you identified your differentiators and the traits that define you. You can use these to develop themes for your presentations. For example:

   5 Ingeniously <u>Practical</u> Ways to Achieve Breakthrough Success

   <u>Spiritual</u> Coaching: Finding Your Compass

3. **Create seasonal topics:** These topics can be used for virtually any group, and you simply adjust your presentation for the particular demographics. Here are some ideas to jump-start your thinking about topics and the kinds of titles you might create for your topics:

New Year's:	*Trade Those Resolutions for Goals and Make Change Happen ... Fast!*
Valentine's:	*Falling in Love with Your Life* (how coaching gets you unstuck)
Spring:	*5 Ways for Making a Fresh Start* (SMART goal-setting)
Summer:	*Use Your Vacation to Change Your Life* (identify goals to set, changes to make)
September:	*Back to the 'School of You'* (what do you want to accomplish?)
Fall:	*Falling Leaves: Time to Let Bad Habits Go* (strategies for changing habits)
Holidays:	*Tightly Wrapped: Unpacking Holiday Stress* (stress reduction strategies)

MARKETING YOUR PRESENTATION

1. **Create a description of your presentation.** Include the title, your name, the fact that you're a life coach, the value proposition for the presentation and a few details. Here's an example:

    How many times have you tried to let go of behaviors and beliefs that aren't working for you any more? And how many times have you succeeded – only to fall right back into old habits? This autumn, it can be different! In the upcoming presentation, *Falling Leaves: Letting Bad Habits Go,* life coach Chris Smith reveals three simple practices for letting go of what's holding you back so you can clear space for fresh opportunities and vibrant new growth.

2. **Put the word out:**

    - **Promote the upcoming event on your website.** There, you can write a longer description and add bullet points to flesh out the details. Make it easy to respond with a phone number, pop-up registration form or a pop-up email reply.

    - **Feature the description on your social media pages.** Be sure to include date, time and how to sign up. Link back to your website.

    - **Send an email to your contacts/client list.** For this list, you'll want to personalize the description: Instead of "life coach Chris Smith reveals," for example, you'd write "I will share ..." You'll also want to end with something like, "I hope to see you there" and a friendly call to action (e.g., "Please let me know if you'll come!").

    - **Send a notice to your local papers.** Local papers love to feature upcoming community activities. Even the local sections of major papers might list your event.

    - **Do a press release that announces the upcoming event.** Link the press release to your website's description of the event. This will help promote the event and raise your search engine visibility. Remember, there are free PR sites you can use.

    - **Tap additional marketing opportunities.** If you're partnering, your partner may also advertise the event (e.g., an announcement in the church bulletin or school newsletter; a memo to employees; a flyer or poster in the waiting room, etc.). You may also be able to use/rent email lists that target your audience (e.g., membership lists for an association or attendee lists for a similar event or conference). Even if there is a fee for the list, it may be worthwhile if you're promoting an event for which you'll charge a fee.

PREPARING FOR YOUR PRESENTATION

Now that you've picked a topic, planned the content and started marketing your event, it's time to start preparing for the actual presentation. Here is a checklist to help you mentally walk through the entire process so you can foresee what you need and anticipate how you'll handle different aspects of the presentation.

Presentation

- **Is it polished and proofread?** It's an awful feeling to see a small typo blown up large on a screen in front of a room full of people! If you're presenting a PowerPoint® make sure you have someone else proof it to double check for errors. Make sure the graphics and grammar reflect your personal brand and professionalism. You do not want a poorly crafted presentation to undermine your credibility and the impact of your message.

- **Have you timed it?** Rehearse it completely – at least three times. You don't want to run through content and have awkward 'dead time' at the end. Nor do you want to go too slowly and then have to race to finish. You might even want to highlight a few areas that could be cut if you do find yourself running long ... and you might want to add a few questions at the end that you can pose to attendees if your main presentation runs a little short.

- **Does it have a STAR moment?** STAR stands for *Something They'll Always Remember.*

  One coach, for example, was doing a presentation on beliefs that hold us back. At the start of the presentation, a backpack sat beside the podium. The first belief she discussed was 'I don't deserve.' When she finished with that discussion, she reached into the backpack and pulled out a big rock and set it down. One by one, as she addressed more beliefs that hold us back, she took rocks out of the backpack and the pile grew. At the very end of her presentation, we all thought the backpack was empty and that she'd already made her point. But then she went again to the backpack. She reached inside and pulled out a pair of running shoes with glittery silver wings attached to them. On each wing were the words 'SOAR!' "My goodness," she laughed. "Who knew I had these all along!" It was stagey, corny, silly ... and utterly unforgettable. The audience clapped like crazy. Years later, we remember that coach and her message about letting go of beliefs that weigh us down so that we can soar.

  A STAR moment doesn't need to involve props. It can be purely visual: you could show a barren hillside followed by an image of that same hillside bursting with yellow daffodils. This could become your theme – a STAR moment that you carry through the entire presentation. At the end, you might add on by giving a daffodil bulb to each attendee as you sum up your presentation.

  The point is to find a STAR moment that works for your own branding, topic and comfort zone.

Location

- **Is the location the right size for the number of people planning to attend?** You don't want people to feel crowded (seems like you didn't plan well). And you don't want a few people scattered through a huge space (seems like the event's a flop before it starts). If registration isn't going as planned, see if you can adjust the arrangements to 'right size' the space.

- **Will you need signage to direct people to the event?** Hotels and office suites generally do a good job of directing guests. But if you're meeting within an organization (library, church, business, etc.) it can be a good idea to come ready with a few posters pointing the way to your specific meeting room.

- **What needs to be on hand**? Will you want to have coffee, tea and water? Will you want attendees to have pens? Do you need a projector or screen? Close your eyes and think through the event: imagine people arriving, entering the room, sitting down, etc. and anticipate what's needed.

Materials

- **What do you need in terms of your presentation?** Will you need to bring your laptop (if so, also be sure to bring your charger). Will you use any props or other aids?

- **Will you provide handouts for attendees?** If so, make sure you have more copies than the number of attendees who register, just in case.

- **What other materials will you want to have on hand?** What about business cards and brochures? Will you be offering books for sale? Will you want to send attendees off with an Action Plan so you have a reason to check back with them in a few weeks?

Preparing yourself

- **What will make you feel confident?** It might be scoping out the location ahead of time. Or knowing exactly where the room is and how long it will take you to travel to the location. Knowing you've done your homework, rehearsed and have all the materials you need will help you look calm and in charge. Some speakers also go through the attendee list ahead of time to familiarize themselves with the names of people who will be in the audience.

- **How will you dress?** Again, go back to your personal brand and think about your traits. If your brand is friendly and approachable, don't wear a severe black suit. If you're practical, don't wear something too trendy or trailing. If you're most at ease in soft fabrics, don't suddenly choose to wear a stiff button-down Oxford shirt. Instead, find something that's polished and professional, but that feels like *you*. Many speakers also suggest dressing in layers so that you can adapt to a room that's chilly or warm.

- **In planning how you'll speak and behave, remember your Comfort Zone.** Be you. Be true to your strengths. If you're a naturally quiet person, make sure you have a good microphone so you can be heard without talking in an unnaturally loud voice. But ... do use strong, confident body language.

  A word about 'Power Poses.' Power Poses are strong, open ways of sitting and standing that convey confidence and authority. Researchers like Harvard's Amy Cuddy have done studies showing that people who use power poses are perceived very differently than those who use more closed positions. In one study, job applicants were divided into two groups. One group simply interviewed. The other group interviewed after spending two minutes in the bathroom doing power poses. The interviewers never saw the bathroom power poses, but they did see the applicants from that group as more desirable – offering this group jobs at a far higher rate than the group that hadn't done the poses. So, as a speaker, it wouldn't hurt to do a little warm up out of sight before starting your presentation!

- **Know your audience and what matters to them.** This is critical because a good presenter talks TO the audience rather than ABOUT a topic. Keep this in mind and your audience will feel your empathy and connection with them.

- **Get personal.** Use examples – draw from your own experience. Tell stories. Doing this every so often grounds your presentation and gives it texture and real-life meaning.

- **Maintain your energy.** This is so important! When YOU stay interested, vibrant and passionate, your audience stays engaged. Plus, you'll seem more confident, experienced and valuable to your audience.

- **Engage your audience by asking questions.** Ask them to predict what will happen in a situation – even if it's obvious. This keeps them talking and actively involved in what you're saying and the points you're making.

- **Make eye contact.** Look at different people while you let ideas sink in. Look at someone and smile. The more you interact with your audience, the more they trust you and value the experience.

FOLLOWING UP YOUR PRESENTATION

Keep track of the people who've attended your event – and keep in touch! Add them to your list of contacts/prospects and continue to follow up throughout the year. In addition, here are a few follow-up steps to take in the first few months after your event.

Right after the presentation: Send an email note to all your attendees thanking them for coming, participating and making the experience so pleasurable. Offer to answer any questions they might have as they think back over the event and urge them to contact you.

If you've handed out an action plan: As discussed earlier, handing out something like a 14-day action plan is a great way to end an event. Attendees have a practical tool for putting what you've discussed into action ... and *you* have a reason to get back in touch with them. Send an email along the lines of: "I wanted to circle back with you and see how you're doing with the action plan. A few attendees have been so excited with the changes they've been able to make, while others haven't had a chance to get started. I'm happy to help in any way you'd like – and I'm always here to answer any questions you may have." This keeps you in touch and makes it easy for the person to say, "As a matter of fact, I'm having trouble getting started. Could you coach me?"

Three months after the presentation: Send an email note to all your attendees. Share any feedback you've had as other attendees have put the ideas of the event into action. Share several more things that work in this particular area and suggest one *further* thing people can do (e.g., another secret of goal-setting, another way to reduce stress, etc.). This paints the picture of you at work coaching others ... and the fact that you can share other success strategies in personal coaching sessions.

SECTION 7:
SEARCH

SEARCH ENGINES AND OPTIMIZATION

As a coach, the majority of your business is likely to come from personal contacts, networking and referrals. Even so, you need a website for visibility and validation. Plus, you want your name and website to be among the top results when people search for coaching services.

That means knowing something about search engine optimization (SEO). Note that we've said *'something,'* not 'everything.' That's because search engines like Google, Bing and Yahoo! are constantly updating their algorithms. In fact, some previously gold-standard SEO tactics for getting to the top of search rankings will now get you penalized and pushed to the bottom.

If you're serious about ranking well, getting the help of an SEO professional can be an excellent investment. It cuts the time and guesswork out of what to do. These experts are especially important for handing technical things that affect SEO, like the structure of your website, meta data and alt tags, and analyzing traffic and engagement.

There are also some tactics you can do yourself. These SEO basics still work and will continue to serve you no matter how quickly search engine algorithms change:

1. **Opt for a website platform you can manage yourself.** WordPress, for instance, makes it easy to add, update and categorize content without knowing how to code. Here, as an example, is a screen shot of a WordPress 'Post' page.

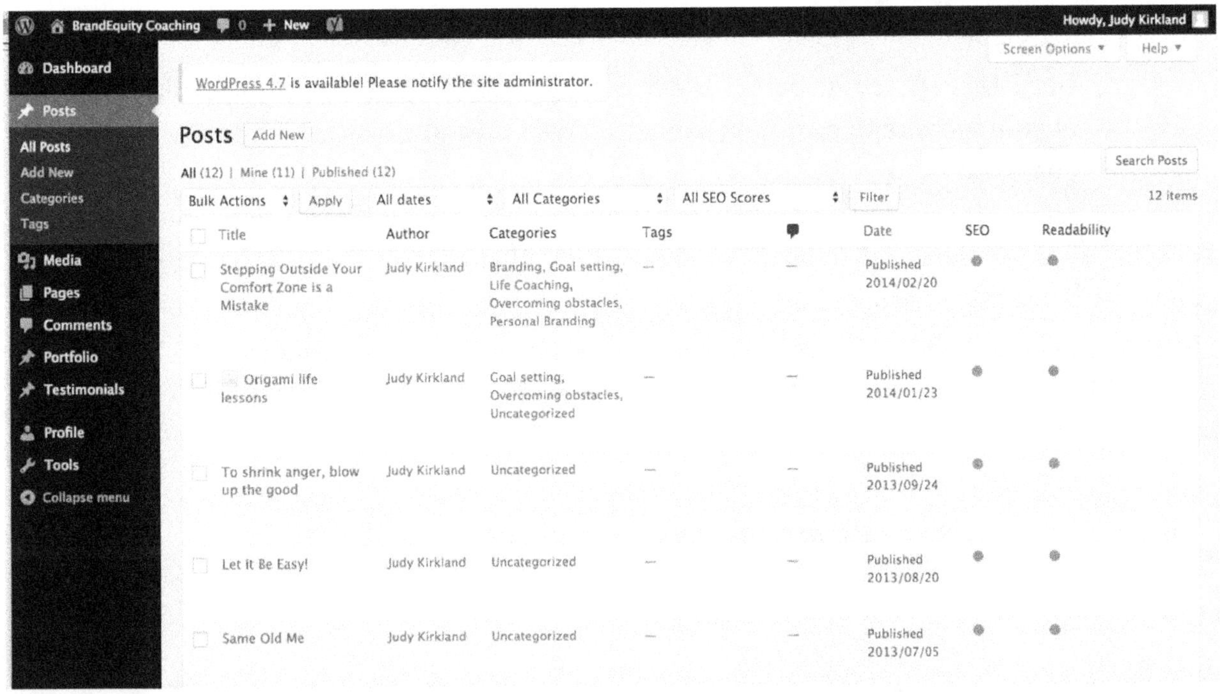

2. **Focus on content.** Because of your personal branding, you'll be very clear about what you do and the story you want to tell. Use this clarity to create content for your site: make sure that every bit of text, every image and every link focuses on this story and helps you tell it. Don't try to tell the story of coaching in general. Don't try to be all things to all people. The more specific you are in targeting your audience and telling your story, the better search engines will understand and the higher they'll rank you in *relevant* searches.

3. **Avoid 'thin content' on your website.** You may like things clean and concise. That's fine, as long as your pages don't seem sparse and overly lightweight. This can signal search engines that it's not worth bringing searchers to your site. Here are few ways to avoid thin content:

   - **All main pages in your website should contain 300-500 words.** Instead of long, wordy paragraphs:
     - Break text into small chunks
     - Let the webpage scroll down deeply (this is a change from earlier SEO tactics)
     - Alternate photos/graphics with short paragraphs, bullet points, captions, etc.
   - **Keep content helpful, original and relevant.** Search engines know if you've picked up language, photos, etc. from another online source. They penalize sites with duplicate content and push the ranking down.
   - **Do not overuse keywords.** Just a while back, packing your site with keywords was the way to rank high. Today's smarter search engines don't like this kind of manipulation and will penalize sites with excessive and unnatural use of keywords. Best advice: write your content naturally. Then, make sure keywords like coaching, life coach and your location are included, but not over-used.

How does *your* content stack up?

Use Siteliner® to find out. Siteliner is a free online tool that lets you look at your website to spot 'thin content' issues such as duplicate content and broken links.

4. **Use captions on photos or diagrams.** Label everything that goes into your content – including graphics and images. This helps with SEO and it helps engage site visitors. This is also an effective way to include keywords. Even if you use stock photos, the caption makes them relevant to your specific practice. E.g., this could be a caption for a life wheel diagram or a photo:

"During our very first coaching session, work-life balance can start to come into focus, along with steps to improve it."

5. **Include a call to action on EVERY page.** Statistics on web traffic show that most people visit just two pages. If those two pages don't happen to be the home page and contact page, you still want people to be able to engage with you. Make sure every page (even blog posts) have a FREE CONSULTATION button. Blog posts should also include SHARE buttons.

6. **Use plug-ins to optimize content.** There are a variety of WordPress plug-ins that *automatically* improve SEO on your web pages, posts and even the images you post. Some of these plug-ins are free. The products and versions change rapidly. Right now, the most popular of the 'beginner-friendly' plug-ins include: WordPress SEO by Yoast, All In One SEO Pack, and WP Social SEO Booster (free and works well with Yoast and All in One).

7. **Refresh your website regularly.** Having a blog page on your site is a great way to do this. Just make sure you also update the *home page* every other month or so. Ideas:
   - List new coaching sessions, pricing or packages
   - Feature a short tip of the month
   - List places you will be speaking or coaching (or where you've appeared/what you've done recently)
   - Post an observation or a conversation-starter on a coaching topic
   - Write up a short case study (never reveal names or identifying information)
   - Examples of results or outcomes of coaching
   - Personal experiences that relate to coaching (perhaps a 'Before and After' of how a situation is handled before and after coaching)

8. **Links still work, but 'Likes' and sharing matter even more.** Although algorithms have cracked down on links, having links coming to and from your website still raises credibility and ranking. Just make sure *search engines see them as natural links* vs. artificial links created only to raise search rankings. Natural links connect to and from sites that offer content that complements your practice, helps educate prospective coaching clients, etc. Having your site shared on social media, however, is even more important. Make sure your website features those easy-share buttons to social media.

Social Sharing: An Easy Short Cut

When you post new material or a blog on your website, copy the URL of that published page and drop it into Facebook, Twitter or LinkeIn and hit 'share.' Automatically, the title, image and a bit of the blog's content will populate your social media post, along with a link back to the full post on your website.

9. **Know when to create a separate landing page.** First, what is a landing page and how is it different from the pages on your website?

    - A landing page is separate from (but can link to) your main website.
    - Landing page content is set up specifically to follow up on an ad or search result.
    - There is limited navigation. Include the offer, audience-specific home page and a click-through to a lead capture form (e.g. receive a report, call to schedule an appointment, receive a free consultation, etc.). You should include links to your main website (Home, Contact, About), but these should be down at the bottom to keep visitors focused on the engagement offered here at the landing page.
    - By monitoring traffic to this site (the click-through rate), you can judge the ad's success.

    If you decide to do an ad campaign *(online ad, social media ad or clickable search result),* you want to target that ad with highly specific keywords, capture information and even have visitors engage with a special offer. Because of this, you don't necessarily want to send people to your home page. Instead, consider creating a landing page that links directly from the ad.

    If you offer different types of coaching services, you may want to create different landing pages. For example, suppose you help people with their work performance. Suppose you also offer help starting a new chapter after life events like divorce or retirement. Clearly, these are two very different stories to tell. We know that trying to tell different stories in one website makes it hard for search engines to understand what you're about – and to rank you well. Consider labeling these types of services (e.g., Performance Coaching and Personal Coaching), mention them briefly on your main website and link to landing pages for each.

10. **Know when to seek help.** In terms of tracking traffic, you may be comfortable using tools like Google Analytics and Siteliner. You may even be comfortable adding WordPress plug-ins and refreshing website content regularly. But while there are many things you can do on your own, launching a Google AdWords campaign and creating a campaign landing page probably aren't among them.

    Investing in professional help from SEO experts can end up saving you money and *making* you money. Most communities offer organizations that help small businesses with marketing and you may find someone willing to give you an hour of time to advise you on getting the biggest impact from your search budget. And, if AdWords is right for your specific life coaching practice, they can help determine what keywords to buy and how to set up the proper links between your landing page and the ad.

ONLINE BUSINESS DIRECTORIES

Online business directories offer an easy – and for the most part free – way to get local exposure for your coaching practice. This provides two benefits: (1) Your practice will be displayed in search results when people search for a coach in your geographic area; and (2) Search engines see multiple listings as a sign of a credible business and this can raise visibility for your listings (including Facebook and LinkedIn) *and* for your website.

- **List your practice in local and national business directories.** Many of these business directories offer free basic listings, with paid upgrades to boost your visibility. There are hundreds of business directories. Here is a starting point for the directories that make the most sense for your coaching practice:

First Priority	**Second Priority**	**Third Priority**
Google/Google+	Better Business Bureau	YP.com
Bing	Merchant Circle	Whitepages
Yahoo!	Local.com	Superpages.com
Yelp	Manta	Patch
Facebook	CitySearch	
LinkedIn	Mojo Pages	
LifeCoachHub.com	YouTube	
(Local Chamber of Commerce)	YouTube	
(The organization from which you earned your certification)		

- **Write a slightly different business description for each directory.** This keeps search engines from seeing the same boilerplate over and over and downgrading your search result rankings for duplicate content. You can use your 25-word description as the core, just switch it up for different directories. BUT: *always keep your business address absolutely consistent anywhere you list it on the Web. This is important because differences could hurt your credibility with search engines.*

SECTION 8:
SMART ACTION PLAN
FOR MARKETING YOUR LIFE COACHING PRACTICE

By now, you understand these key concepts:

1. Marking your practice effectively starts with your personal brand.

2. Your marketing plan will be uniquely yours, not a templated marketing plan.

3. It will feel comfortable because it will be geared to your specific strengths, approach to coaching, bandwidth and budget.

4. It will cover tactics that fall into these categories:
   a. Basic tools
   b. Engagement
   c. Networking
   d. Social Media
   e. Events
   f. Search

You also understand what types of tactics to consider and how to decide when – and whether – you'll use them. Bottom line: you've covered a lot of ground! But you still don't have a marketing plan. That's what this next section will help you create.

First, we'll summarize the categories and **the one-time marketing efforts** we've discussed into the single At-A-Glance Chart on the following page. Isn't it a relief to see all the elements of your entire basic toolkit all pulled together on a single page? Things are beginning to look simpler already!

Next, we'll show you how to start executing these projects, step-by-step and on a timeline that won't add extra stress to your already busy schedule.

Then, we'll use the same process to map out a plan for what to do each month to keep your life coaching practice visible, valuable and growing.

Let's start using this process now to create a marketing plan that amplifies your earnings and simplifies your success!

1x Time Efforts	Specific	Measurable	Action	Reasonable	Time	Cost
BASIC TOOLS	Website	5-page site	Follow guide on pg. 22	Get domain URL Get site hosting Create content	0.5 hr 0.5 hr 3 hrs	$15/yr $0-240/yr DIY $0*
	Business Cards	500 2-sided cards	Choose vendor	Create content Upload content	1 hr 1 hr	$30-100
	Elevator Pitch	10- & 45-second pitches	Do workbook exercise on pg. 16	Write 10/45 pitch Memorize/rehearse	1 hr 1 hr	$0 $0
	Brochure	PDF 2-sided flyer (print on demand)	Follow guide on pgs. 24-25	Complete content Buy stock photos Flow into format	2 hrs 1 hr 1 hr	DIY $0* $20+
	Business Description	Ready-to-use 25 words	Follow guide on pg. 19	Write business description	1 hr	$0
ENGAGEMENT	Create value propositions and offers	Define audiences, pricing, packaging and guarantee	Follow guide on pg. 29	Create offer statements	2 hrs	$0
	Create give-aways for your audiences	Brainstorm ideas	Use examples on pg. 33	Develop 1 giveaway	1 hr	DIY $0*
	Create contact file	Spreadsheet/table: prospects/clients	Use sample fields on pg. 34	Enter current contacts	2 hrs	DIY $0
NETWORKING	Define networking tactics	Explore casual and professional opportunities	Do the exercises on pgs. 39-40	Write out steps needed to pursue these opportunities	1 hr	$0 + up for orgs. & events
	Be ready to follow up leads	Find/write 2 articles	Follow the guide on pg. 50	Turn the articles into PDFs, ready to print or email	1 hr	$0
SOCIAL MEDIA	Establish your social media presence	Set up Facebook and LinkedIn pages	Follow the guide on pg. 55	Invite FB friends to LIKE your page Start adding LinkedIn contacts	2 hrs	$0
	Create a content strategy	Develop an editorial plan for FB and LI	Use the planner on pg. 62	Write your initial 2 posts for FB	2 hrs	$0
EVENTS	Create an events strategy	Will you test an event? What it will be?	Use the guidance starting on pg. 66	If doing an event, define promo tactics (pg. 68)	1 hr	$0
	Prepare a presentaion	If you're doing an event, plan it	Use the guidance starting on pg. 67	Tally costs/items to assemble	2 hrs	$0*
SEARCH	Get search-visible	Choose business directories	Use the sources on pg. 77	Upload 25-word biz description	1 hr	$0+ fees for some
	Create a press release	Announce your practice	Use the sample format on pg. 27	Post release: free and/or paid sites	2 hrs	
				Total Estimated Cost for Basic Tools plus 1 year of hosting and domain		**$305+***

*The costs here are for 'doing it yourself'. Extra costs are associated with purchasing services or items.

By listing out your one-time efforts, you know the specific steps required to build your basic toolkit, and you know how long each step will take. Accomplishing the total plan will take about 30 hours.

To get started, look at your calendar and begin slotting in when you will work on a particular step (use the TIME estimates to help you find the right-sized project for specific days, depending on how busy you are). How you invest those 30 hours is completely flexible for your own personal bandwidth:

- Allot 1 hour a day and complete your Basic Toolkit in 30 days
- Allot 1 hour a week and complete your Basic Toolkit in 30 weeks – about 7 months

The pace is up to you. The point is that no matter what kind of time you can invest in these one-time efforts, you can lay the entire foundation of a strong marketing program for your practice.

Before you begin to slot in specific times on your calendar, use a grid like this to help map out the activities. The sample below shows how to accomplish all one-time efforts by **investing just 5 hours a week**.

	BASIC TOOLS	ENGAGEMENT	NETWORKING	SOCIAL MEDIA	EVENTS	SEARCH
WEEK 1	Create and order biz cards (2 hrs) Biz description (1 hr)			Set up FB and LI pages, invite friends (2 hrs)		
WEEK 2	Elevator Pitch (2hrs)	Create offers (2 hrs)				Upload biz description to directories (1 hr)
WEEK 3	Get URL (.5 hr) Get site (.5 hr)	Create contact file (2 hrs)	Define networking tactics (1 hr)		Events strategy (1 hr)	
WEEK 4	Create Web content (3 hrs)			Create content plan, write 2 posts (2 hrs)		
WEEK 5	Create brochure (4 hrs)		Find/prepare articles for lead follow up (1 hr)			
WEEK 6		Develop giveaway concept (1 hr)			Plan a presentation (2 hrs)	Press release announcing your practice (2 hrs)

You've mapped out the first section of your SMART marketing plan. Very soon, you'll have your Basic Toolkit in place and foundational activities underway.

Now, on to the next step: **mapping out the recurring action items**. Again, we'll use a two-step approach to break down *what* needs to be done and *how* everything will get done. Start by using the format below. We've entered most of the information, but there are areas where you'll need to define the specific activities you've chosen. For those, enter the type of information indicated in the italic text.

RECURRING ACTIVITIES	SPECIFIC	MEASURABLE	ACTION	ACTION	TIME
ENGAGEMENT	Continue to expand the contact file	Collect new contact information	Keep the list current	Add/remove/update information regularly	1x month
	Use file to stay in touch with contacts	Plan topics or news to share with contacts	Send notes/ emails to your contact file	Strive to send quarterly messages to contacts	4x year
NETWORKING	Attend networking event(s)	*Define your activities*	*Enter details on days, times*	*Set goal for how often you'll attend*	*Define frequency*
	Follow up on leads	Reach out to new/ existing contacts	Send articles to new contacts; notes to existing	Turn the articles into PDFs, ready to print or email	*Frequency = same as above)*
SOCIAL MEDIA	Stay current and active on Facebook and LinkedIn	Create regular posts	Strive for 4 posts per month	Post weekly	4x month
EVENTS	Speak or hold an event	*Define the specific event: org., topic*	*Enter details on day, time, location*	Prepare promotional and logistical activities	*milestones: e.g., 1 week ahead, confirm # attendees*
	Stay in touch with attendees	Send follow up	Check in with them/with *XX-day* plan	Strive to start conversations about follow-on coaching with at least 20% of attendees	Follow up with all attendees within *[define your timeframe]*
SEARCH	Implement a Search Engine Optimization strategy/program	*Depends on your search strategy*	*Depends on your search strategy*	*Depends on your search strategy*	*Depends on your search strategy*
	Raise organic search visibility	Use press releases	Strive to send quarterly releases	Post the release on free and/or paid PR sites, also as email attachment to your contact list as appropriate with note about your news	4x year

As with the one-time efforts, slot these recurring activities into a monthly "to do" list like this:

	ENGAGEMENT	NETWORKING	SOCIAL MEDIA	EVENTS	SEARCH
JAN	Update contacts Send seasonal 'touch' to leads/ clients (see pg. 35)	Attend event: *add date, time, etc.* Lead follow-up	Post every Tuesday	Host event: Trade Resolutions for Goals: *add date, time, etc.*	Run Google Analytics to benchmark web traffic, pages seen
FEB	Update contacts	Attend event: *add date, time, etc.* Lead follow-up	Post every Tuesday Offer a giveaway report/guide	Send event follow-up to attendee	Post a press release (could relate to giveaway)
MAR	Update contacts	Attend event: *add date, time, etc.* Lead follow-up	Post every Tuesday	Plan next event: topics/audience	*SEO activities per guidance of outside firm, if used*
APR	Update contacts Email leads/clients	Attend event: *add date, time, etc.* Lead follow-up	Post every Tuesday	Reserve location for event	Refresh web homepage, update site content
MAY	Update contacts	Attend event: *add date, time, etc.* Lead follow-up	Post every Tuesday (include 1 on upcoming event)	Start promo activities	Send Press Release about the event
JUN	Update contacts	Attend event: *add date, time, etc.* Lead follow-up	Post every Tuesday (include 1 on upcoming event)	Prepare presentation Continue promo	Update homepage with info about event
JUL	Update contacts	Attend event: *add date, time, etc.* Lead follow-up	Post every Tuesday (include 1 on upcoming event)	Rehearse presentation Continue promo	Update website with any new memberships, topics, etc.
AUG	Update contacts Send seasonal 'touch' to leads/ clients (see pg. 35)	Attend event: *add date, time, etc.* Lead follow-up	Post every Tuesday (include 1 on upcoming event)	Tally attendance, materials needed, etc.	Send press release on 'news' (topic ideas p. 26)
SEP	Update contacts	Attend event: *add date, time, etc.* Lead follow-up	Post every Tuesday	Host event: Trade Resolutions for Goals: *add date, time, etc.*	Send press following up on the event: attendees, etc.
OCT	Update contacts	Attend event: *add date, time, etc.* Lead follow-up	Post every Tuesday	Plan next event: topics/audience	Review online directory listings, update as needed
NOV	Update contacts email leads/clients	Attend event: *add date, time, etc.* Lead follow-up	Post every Tuesday	Reserve location for event	Refresh web homepage, update site content
DEC	Update contacts	Attend event: *add date, time, etc.* Lead follow-up	Post every Tuesday	Start promo activities	Send Press Release about the event

As with the one-time efforts, the final step is transferring this to-do list to your calendar. **DO NOT SKIP THIS STEP!** As a life coach you know that deciding 'when' makes all the difference in following through.

LOOK AT WHAT YOU'VE ACCOMPLISHED!

You've not only become a life coach, you've now created a plan for building a vibrant and growing practice. It's a plan that will feel comfortable because it's designed specifically for who you are, your strengths, your vision of coaching, your budget and your bandwidth. It's also a plan that will work for you! Follow through on these one-time efforts and recurring action items and you're virtually guaranteed to see results.

It's worth the investment it takes to create your plan. That's because a strong plan becomes your path to a practice that rewards you with more income and more opportunities to help people. How satisfying. How meaningful. And with this step-by-step approach, how easy!

Congratulations!

ABOUT THE AUTHORS

JUDY KIRKLAND is an author, Certified Life Coach and nationally known specialist in content creation and business and personal branding. During her 30-year marketing career, Judy has created award-winning websites and campaigns promoting everything from grassroots advocacy, charities and membership, to healthcare practices, investment advisories, telecommunications firms, and publishers. In 2013, she co-founded The LiveWell Institute, which develops a variety of resources for helping people live well, even through life's most challenging chapters. Her BrandEquity Coaching program, *Plan BE: Using Who You Already Are to Live the Life You've Always Dreamed* is available through The LiveWell Institute for life coaches to use as the basis for group seminars and multi-session private coaching programs.

SUSAN WEAVER is a Certified Life Coach, Certified Grief Counselor and Reiki Master practitioner. Since 1997, Susan has owned a successful Washington, DC-area marketing agency that specializes in integrating email, social media, online and print tactics into award-winning campaigns for clients who range from solo entrepreneurs to Fortune 100 businesses. She is the author of the acclaimed *Rainbow Reach* book series for helping children deal with grief and anxiety. With Judy, Susan co-founded The LiveWell Institute to help people of every age unlock their creativity, compassion and ability to make a difference. Programs and materials based on her *Rainbow Reach* series are available through The LiveWell Institute for use by therapists and life coaches.

ABOUT THE LIVEWELL INSTITUTE

SIMPLE STEPS TO DRAMATIC IMPROVEMENTS

The LiveWell Institute was founded in 2013 to help individuals of all ages discover how to use their immediate *power of self-awareness* to create happy and healthy changes in their lives. How can such dramatic improvements come from simple self-awareness?

The POWER of Self-awareness

Self-awareness creates confidence. It provides the knowledge necessary to bring about positive change and positive attitude. **Positive people are happier.** Happy people treat themselves *and others* with care and respect that can be handed down from generation to generation, creating happier families and workplaces, and a happier world in which to live – for ourselves, our children, and our grandchildren.

You don't have to be a natural: whether you're 5 or 95, you can *learn* to shine and to share, collaborate, laugh, thrive, persevere and bounce back. You can learn how to get unstuck – freed from beliefs, habits and burdens that have weighed you down, stressed you out and left you defenseless against discord and disease.

LiveWell teaches these skills: using our **AWAKE self-awareness methodology**. Our workshops and books focus on practical ways to 'wake up' to new ways to live well and to *make a difference.*

While Kindergarteners are learning to count, they learn to count their blessings. Couples and families live extraordinary lives by simply living their values. Individuals feel healthier inside and out. And organizations and communities trade stress, in-fighting and mediocrity for vibrant teamwork, clarity and excellence in dreaming bigger dreams – and realizing them, faster.

Our programs create the greatest reach and rewards for everyone. Our ready-to-present workshops can be licensed and used effectively by schools, HR directors, parishes, life coaches, wellness coaches, business consultants, therapists ... anyone who wants to teach. The thinking is already there, the presentations are well-researched and entertaining, and our facilitator guides provide even first-timers the know-how and confidence to present like pros.

Only LiveWell workshops feature AWAKE. No other program features LiveWell's exclusive AWAKE self-awareness methodology. Each presentation is built on the best work in its field – from wellness and stress management, to goal setting and team building. Instead of simply presenting positivity concepts, all presentations use the AWAKE approach (Attention, What's working, Awareness, Knowing and Energy) to coach audiences beyond *learning* these life-changing skills to *living* them. It's a difference that gives presenters real power to *make a difference.*

INDEX

A
Action Plan, 33–34, 70, 72
apps, 55, 60

B
balance, work/life, 49
blog, 56, 75
blog posts, 75
brainstorm, 2–3, 39, 57, 62–63
brand identity, 12–13
brand traits, 6–7, 30
brochure, 6, 9–10, 24–25, 30, 70, 80
brochure templates, 25
business bio, 9–10
business cards, 9, 11, 13–14, 46, 49, 70
business description, 18–19, 77, 80
business directories, 77, 80
business name, 22, 25, 59
business owners, women, 53–54
business profile, 55

C
captions, 21–22, 74
careers, 28, 45, 48–49
casual networking, 37–39
clients, potential, 27, 31
clubs, 38–41
coaches, 1, 10, 31–32, 35, 38, 53, 56–57, 60, 64–65, 69, 72–73, 77
coaching certifications, 4, 10
coaching niche, 18–19
coaching sessions, 6, 29, 32–34, 42, 74
  personal, 65, 72
coaching topics, 54, 75
colors, 11, 13, 25
comfort zone, 2, 4–6, 15, 38–39, 57, 69, 71
Commerce, 28, 38–39, 50, 77
community groups, 38–39
community organizations, 37–38
contact information, 25, 33–34, 61, 64
CONTACT page, 21–22, 75
contacts, 22–23, 27–28, 37, 48, 50–51, 55, 60, 72, 76, 82
content, 20–21, 24–25, 27, 55–59, 63–64, 69, 74–75, 80
conversations, 15, 41, 43–44, 46, 53, 56, 58, 65
cost, 1, 13–14, 28, 40, 80
credentials, 10, 24–25

D
design, 11–13, 25, 32
designer, professional graphic, 12–13
differentiators, 5–7, 10, 23, 25, 30, 67
directories, 77, 81

E
elevator pitch, 6, 9, 15–17, 42, 80–81
email contact list, 60
engagements, speaking, 10, 18, 33, 38, 65
events, 7, 26, 33, 38, 51, 65–72, 79–83
  group, 65–66
  host, 83
  upcoming, 68, 83
events strategy, 80–81
experience, 1, 10, 22–23, 29, 31, 71–72
exposure, 59–60, 64

F
Facebook, 21–23, 50, 53, 55–56, 58–61, 63–64, 75, 77, 82
Facebook Groups, 53–55
Facebook page, personal, 55–56
fans, 55, 60
FB, 22, 80–81
format, 12–13, 25, 27, 80, 82
fresh start, 48–49, 67

G
giveaways, 29, 33, 80, 83
goals, 1–2, 8, 21–23, 28–33, 35, 41–42, 44, 49, 54, 57, 61, 65, 67, 83
group coaching, 22, 53
groups, 37–39, 43–44, 53, 55–56, 65, 67, 71

H
homepage, 21, 27, 75–76
host, 65–66
hosting, 20, 65–66, 80
hours, 40, 54, 57, 76, 81

I
International Coach Federation, 50

K
keywords, 74, 76

L
landing page, 76
life coaches, certified, 10, 85
life coaching clients, 55
life coaching fees, 31
life coaching sessions, 48
LinkedIn, 50, 55–56, 58, 60–61, 63–64, 77, 82
links, 21–22, 26–27, 55–56, 68, 75–76
LiveWell Institute, 51, 85, 87

M
marketing, 1, 65, 68, 76, 79
marketing plan, 8, 79
materials, 29, 50, 70, 83, 85
members, 37, 53–55, 66–67

N
networking, 5, 7, 15, 35, 37–41, 43–45, 47, 49, 51, 53, 66, 73, 79–83
networking clubs, 37–39
networking event, 46, 53, 82
news, 26–27, 41, 44, 65, 82–83
niche, 18–19, 31–32

O
online printers, 13
Onsite events, 66
organizations, 27, 38–39, 66–67, 70, 76–77, 87

P
partners, 49, 66–68
personal brand, 1, 5–6, 8, 67, 69, 79
personal branding, 1–3, 5, 7, 30, 61, 67, 71, 74, 85
Phone Website, 27
photos, 20–23, 25, 55–56, 58–60, 64, 66, 74
Pinterest, 56, 58–60
planner, editorial content, 60–62
post, 26, 53–58, 60, 63–64, 73, 75, 80–83

posting, 24, 53, 55, 57–59
post videos, 55
presentation, 23, 51, 53, 66–72, 81, 83, 87
press release, 26–27, 68, 80–81, 83
prices, 13, 20, 31–32
pricing, 29, 31–32, 75, 80
printing, 12–13, 46
professional networking clubs, 37, 40, 42, 49

R
referral partners, 24, 49, 51
referrals, 34, 38, 40, 47–48, 53, 65, 73
refreshing website content, 76
rewards, 29–30, 38, 84, 87

S
search, 34, 50, 73, 75, 77, 79–83
search engine optimization. See SEO
search engines, 26–27, 73–74, 76–77
search strategy, 82
SEO (search engine optimization), 73–75, 82
services, online life coach referral, 50
site, 20–21, 23, 50, 56, 58, 74–76, 80–81
SMART Action Plan, 79, 81, 83
SMART GOALS, 8, 42, 57
social media posts, 57, 75
social media sites, 58, 63
solution, 33, 57
STAR, 69
stoppers, 31–33
stories, 1, 7, 20, 64, 71, 74, 76
strengths, 2, 5–6, 10–11, 18, 30, 32, 71, 79, 84
survey, 60

T
templates, 13, 20, 25
TESTIMONIAL page, 21–22
testimonials, 22–23, 25–27
titles, 27–28, 67–68, 75
tools, basic, 9, 79–81
Twitter, 56, 58, 60, 63, 75

U
update contacts, 83

V
value proposition, 23, 29–32, 67–68
videos, 20, 55–56, 61, 64
visibility, 26, 29, 38, 46, 55–56, 64–65, 73, 77
vision, 15–17, 25, 54, 84

W
website, main, 76
Website Assessment Tool for Life Coaches, 23
website design, 7
website features, 20, 75
words, 4, 6, 18–19, 27, 29, 34, 50, 68–69, 71, 74, 80

Y
YouTube, 22, 55–56, 58–59, 61, 77
YouTube Channel, 55

CPSIA information can be obtained
at www.ICGtesting.com
Printed in the USA
LVHW061133130119
603750LV00017B/1329/P

9 780991 059249